Vanguard of Valor
Volume II

Small Unit Actions in Afghanistan

General Editor
Donald P. Wright, Ph. D.

Afghan Study Team Authors
Anthony E. Carlson, Ph. D.

Michael J. Doidge

Scott J. Gaitley

Kevin M. Hymel

Matt M. Matthews

Ryan D. Wadle, Ph. D.

Editing and Layout
Terry D. England

Carl W. Fischer

Deborah J. Seed

Graphics
Robin D. Kern

Foreword

Beginning in 2009, the United States and many of its NATO-ISAF partners dramatically raised their levels of effort in Afghanistan. The "Afghan Surge," as it came to be known, was most evident in the number of additional US and allied troops that arrived in Afghanistan in 2009 and 2010. Their mission was clear: To reverse the Taliban's momentum and deny it the ability to overthrow the government, and to strengthen the capacity of Afghanistan's security forces and government so that they could assume lead responsibility for their nation's future.

For US Army units, the ways of creating stability and furthering the reach of the Afghan Government took several forms. First and foremost, US Soldiers executed complex and difficult offensive operations to seize territory that had often been held by insurgents for years. These combat actions were often complemented by civic action projects that were carried out together with US diplomats and development specialists. Additionally, US Soldiers formed close partnerships with Afghan Army and Police units to accelerate the growth of the Afghan security forces' capabilities.

At the heart of all of these efforts were the men and women who served in front line units during what has become longest war in our Nation's history. In my time as the senior US commander in Afghanistan and as US Ambassador to that country, I recognized that the success of the campaign depended greatly on the skill, valor, and grit of our Army Soldiers. This was true especially of the sergeants, lieutenants, and captains who make critical decisions under stressful combat conditions and interact on a regular basis with Afghan Soldiers and civilians.

The present volume, Vanguard of Valor II, offers six accounts of US Soldiers at the tip of the spear during the Afghan campaign. The Combat Studies Institute's Vanguard of Valor series is intended to document small unit actions in Afghanistan. These books play an equally important role by offering insights to Soldiers who may find themselves in the years ahead under similar conditions, whether in Afghanistan or in some other troubled land where they have been deployed to conduct the dangerous business of defending the national interest in a theater of war.

Karl W. Eikenberry
Ambassador and Lieutenant General
 US Army (Retired)
Stanford University

Acknowledgements

This volume of the Vanguard of Valor series continues the Combat Studies Institute's effort to document small unit actions in Afghanistan. The study of these actions afford leaders the opportunity to better prepare themselves for continued operations in Afghanistan and for future conflicts yet to be determined by our nation's interests.

Mr. Robert J. Dalessandro, Chief of Military History, and Dr. Richard W. Stewart, Chief Historian of the Army, were instrumental in the production of this book. Their continued vision and support of CSI as a publisher of contemporary military history allowed us to complete this volume. I also wish to acknowledge the numerous Command Historians, Military History Detachments, and the Operational Leadership Experiences' oral history interviewers for their collection efforts over the past decade; without them this volume would not have been possible. I extend special acknowledgement and thanks to the Soldiers who provided interviews and first-hand accounts of the events about which these writings document.

The Afghan Study Team continues its work on the study of operations and unit actions in Afghanistan. Future volumes will focus not only on small units actions but will expand to examine battalion, brigade, and divisional level operations. We will continue telling the story of Soldiers serving on distant and difficult battlefields.

CSI – The Past is Prologue!

Roderick M. Cox
Colonel, US Army
Director, Combat Studies Institute

Contents

Foreword .... *iii*

Acknowledgements .... *v*

Contents .... *vii*

List of Figures .... *ix*

Geographical Key to Operations Recounted in this Work .... *xi*

Chapter 1. Toe to Toe with the Taliban
Bravo Company Fights in Makuan
*   by Kevin M. Hymel* *1*

Chapter 2. Gaining the Initiative in Musahi
Using CERP to Disrupt the Taliban in Kabul Province
*   by Anthony E. Carlson, Ph. D.* *29*

Chapter 3. Partnership in Paktika Province, 2010-2011
*   by Ryan D. Wadle, Ph.D.* *55*

Chapter 4. Leading the Charge
A Cavalry Platoon's Fight in Badghis Province
*   by Matt M. Matthews* *79*

Chapter 5. Combat Multipliers
Tactical Female Engagement Teams in Paktika Province
*   by Michael J Doidge* *105*

Chapter 6. Securing Dan Patan
A US Infantry Squad's Counterinsurgency Program in an Afghan District
*   by Scott J. Gaitley* *125*

Glossary *147*

About the Authors *151*

List of Figures

Chapter 1.
    Figure 1. The Makuan Operation, 14-18 September 2010.................. 4
    Figure 2. Assault Breacher Vehicle cuts through grape field............. 5
    Figure 3. IEDs lay partially concealed.. 6
    Figure 4. Soldier conducts a bomb damage assessment.................. 12

Chapter 2.
    Figure 1. Kabul Province and the Musahi District.......................... 32
    Figure 2. The Musahi valley.. 33
    Figure 3. ANP Officer Distributes HA Supplies in Mushai valley .. 39
    Figure 4. Musahi Child Clutches a Blanket Received during HA... 40
    Figure 5. Musahi Taliban Weapons Cache...................................... 44
    Figure 6. Wreckage of the Musahi District Government Center..... 45

Chapter 3.
    Figure 1. Map of Paktika Province.. 58
    Figure 2. Team building dinner for the US and ANA RCPs 67

Chapter 4.
    Figure 1. Badghis Province and Bala Morghab District................. 80
    Figure 2. Red Platoon Operations, 3-4 April, 2011........................ 86
    Figure 3. Conducting SLE in Kamusari 4 April 2011 88
    Figure 4. Forward observer secures a sector of Kamusari Village. 90
    Figure 5. Engage the enemy from OP Reaper 4.............................. 94
    Figure 6. Air Force B-1 Lancer drops a guided bomb.................... 98

Chapter 5.
    Figure 1. Staff Sergeant Denise Ferniza with Afghan children.......113
    Figure 2. Staff Sergeant Ferniza instructs in combat medicine.......119
    Figure 3. Sergeant Ashley Dixon on an engagement 120
    Figure 4. Sergeant Major Joseph Singerhouse with FETs............. 121

Chapter 6.
> *Figure 1. Afghan Local Police sites..128*
> *Figure 2. Dan Patan district geographical reference map............133*

Geographical Key to Operations Recounted in this Work.

Toe to Toe with the Taliban
Bravo Company Fights in Makuan
by
Kevin M. Hymel

Confusion reigned. An improvised explosive device (IED) had just detonated beneath the boot of an American lieutenant, tearing through the men of 2d Platoon. Soldiers screamed and yelled. Those not tossed into the air were thrown to the ground. The device had exploded only 15 minutes after two other IEDs ripped through 3d Platoon, which 2d Platoon was attempting to support. The blasts rendered both platoons ineffective. The Afghan town of Makuan was proving itself a deadly place for the men of Bravo Company, 1st Battalion, 502d Infantry Regiment (1-502d IN), 2d Brigade Combat Team, 101st Airborne Division (Air Assault).

Bravo Company had entered Makuan the previous day to clear the area of IEDs, bomb-making facilities, and insurgents. On this night of 17 September 2010, the Soldiers conducted a clearing operation before they were to head south toward the Arghandab River, one kilometer away. Most of Bravo's noncommissioned officers (NCOs) hated moving through an area strewn with IEDs at night, but they had their orders. Now, in only a few minutes, a clearing operation had become a company commander's nightmare: a mass casualty situation.

The Plan

Bravo Company's mission in Makuan was part of Operation DRAGON STRIKE, a brigade-sized operation designed to clear the Taliban out of Kandahar Province's Zhari District in southeastern Afghanistan. The town of Makuan was located approximately 24 kilometers west of Kandahar, one kilometer south of Highway One, and a kilometer north of the Arghandab River. As the main east-west route between Kandahar to the east and Gereshk to the west, Highway One proved a favorite Taliban target. The Taliban used Makuan as an IED factory, a bed-down area for insurgents moving in and out of Kandahar, and a consolidation position for attacks on Highway One traffic. Protected from the north by a series of IED belts, Makuan contained an active enemy who had driven the civilians out of the area.[1]

Makuan consisted of a series of mud compounds and grape huts surrounded by grape rows, marijuana fields, and pomegranate orchards—some of which were separated by mud walls. The dense terrain resembled the hedgerow country of 1944 Normandy, France. Grape vines stood as tall as a Soldier. "When you step into them, you just disappear," said Captain James "Brandon" Prisock, Bravo Company's commander. A canal ran east-to-west just north of the town, with numerous wadis—dry river beds—running through the area.[2]

To drive the enemy out of Makuan, Lieutenant Colonel Johnny Davis, the 1-502d IN commander, tasked Charlie Company, on the battalion's right flank, with attacking an area eight kilometers northeast of Makuan, east of the city of Senjaray and pushing down to the Arghandab River. Simultaneously, he ordered Alpha Company to attack south out of Senjaray. With these shaping operations distracting the enemy, Bravo Company, a company of US Army Rangers, and an Afghanistan National Army (ANA) company would air-assault south of Makuan. The combined force would advance north, clearing the town of insurgents and IEDs. The surprised enemy would have nowhere to run but north, into the battalion's Delta Company and Headquarters and Headquarters Company, positioned along Highway One. The air assault was set for 12 September 2010.[3]

Bravo Company had been fighting the Taliban along Highway One since late May 2010, engaging the enemy two or three times a day. "We lost a lot of guys in the beginning," said Specialist Jason Leigh, the company radio telephone operator (RTO). "We had a lot of casualties."[4] The company had been split between two Combat Out Posts (COPs) in the village of Pashmul, approximately four kilometers southwest of Makuan. When Bravo transferred to FOB Wilson, northwest of Makuan, the whole unit reunited and received a new commander. Captain Prisock took over Bravo on 5 September, seven days before DRAGON STRIKE's expected kick-off date. He had served a tour in Iraq and helped plan DRAGON STRIKE as a member of the battalion's operations staff. The arrival of a new commander and the unit's consolidation had a profound effect on the men. "Morale changed," explained Captain Luke Rella, the company's executive officer (XO). "People started actually feeling like they were part of a team again, and they really cared about the unit."[5]

Captain Prisock had studied the enemy's tactics. He read The Other Side of the Mountain, a book about mujahideen attacks on Soviets during the Soviet-Afghan War, specifically the section on ambushes along Highway One, north of Makuan. "[The Taliban] were fighting from the exact same positions that [the mujahideen] fought [the Soviets]," explained Prisock. "We noticed that they were fighting in the exact same way."[6]

Captain Prisock's command included three rifle platoons: First Lieutenant Charles Ragland's 1st Platoon, First Lieutenant Taylor

Murphy's 2d Platoon, and First Lieutenant Nicholas Williams' 3d Platoon. All three platoon leaders were on their first combat tour, but their noncommissioned officers were combat veterans. Prisock also had extra assets for his mission: a squad of engineers, an Explosive Ordnance Disposal (EOD) team, a Human Intelligence Collection Team, and the battalion's Advanced Trauma Life Support unit. He also received an Assault Breacher Vehicle platoon from the US Marine Corps; Seabees (engineers) from the US Navy; and bomb-sniffing dogs from both the US Air Force and the Navy. The extra units swelled Bravo Company to the equivalent of nine platoons.[7]

Charlie Company launched its attack on 7 September, "and boy, did they bring out the enemy," said Lieutenant Colonel Davis, "and that set up the conditions for us to push Bravo Company."[8] While Charlie Company engaged the enemy, the men of Bravo Company rehearsed the air assault at FOB Wilson. They were ready, but as the 12 September date drew near, the Rangers were committed to a different mission and a storm front threatened to ground the assault helicopters. The date was pushed back twice until 14 September at 2230, when the men were told to stand down for 48 hours. An hour later, as the Bravo men bedded down, orders came that the operation would kick off in about eight hours. Most of the soldiers were awakened out of their first sleep in days and scrambled to get ready.[9]

The air assault had been cancelled, but with the larger operation already underway, Lieutenant Colonel Davis needed Bravo Company to conduct a ground attack. The men now had eight hours to get themselves to an Afghan National Police (ANP) station five miles northeast on Highway One for the jump-off. "It was a mess," said the company's First Sergeant Nathan Stone, "but we moved." Stone organized the men into chalks, just as he would for an air assault. "We just used our vehicles like helicopters," he explained.[10] Stone placed milk crates where the trucks would arrive. Men lined up and counted off as they mounted the trucks, which then whisked them down Highway One. The trucks then made round trips to pick up other chalks. Some of the soldiers worried that the massive movement would alert the insurgents. "We're definitely tipping our hand [to the enemy] at that point," commented Lieutenant Nicholas Williams.[11] First Sergeant Stone boarded the last truck and arrived at the ANP station just as the company began moving south toward Makuan. "That's how hard we pushed it," he said.[12]

Breaching by MICLIC

Bravo Company did not attack alone. Three US Marine Corps Assault Breacher Vehicles (ABVs), M1 tank chassis fitted with a mine plow and M58 Mine Clearing Line Charges (MICLICs), would breach the enemy lines and eliminate any IEDs awaiting the infantry. Accompanying the ABVs were two M88 Tank Recovery Vehicles, armed with .50-caliber machine guns and IED plows, and a number of Mine Resistant Ambush Protected (MRAP) vehicles. Captain Prisock positioned Bravo Company behind the ABVs. Once the ABVs started rolling forward, the men would advance and protect their flanks.

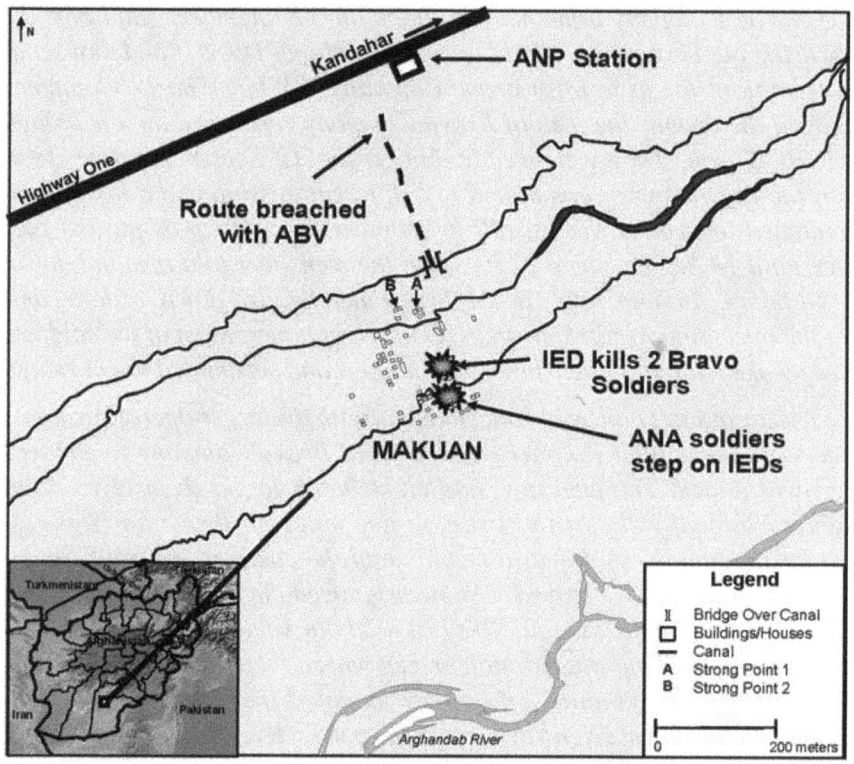

Figure 1. The Makuan Operation, 14-18 September 2010.

As the sun rose on 15 September, one of the ABVs fired a MICLIC, commencing the operation. Like a spider shooting a web, the MICLIC rocket shot out of the ABV as the line charge uncoiled behind it. The rocket arced over the IED-strewn grape field and landed 100 meters away. The line charge then detonated, shaking the earth and raising a huge, long cloud of dirt. Sympathetic detonations added to the power of the explosion. When the dust settled, an eight-meter-wide path had been cut through the IEDs in the grape rows. Everyone remembered the power of the MICLIC. "You can see the earth move in front of you," said Sergeant Zac McDonald.[13] "Those are the loudest things you'll ever hear in your life," added Air Force Staff Sergeant Brent Olson, one of Bravo Company's dog handlers.[14] "Everything feels tight for a minute," explained Staff Sergeant Nicholas Christensen, "[your] ears are ringing, and the dust. It's almost too much to bear, but then it ends quickly."[15] Staff Sergeant Joseph Roberts may have explained the effect best when he said, "It's like a precursor to the things to come."[16] Insurgents began running away from a wadi line just south of the breach. A Soldier in the ANP station's tower, manning a Mark 19 40mm grenade launcher, fired rounds at the exposed enemy while the Marine ABVs opened up with their .50-caliber machine guns.[17]

Figure 2. An Assault Breacher Vehicle (ABV) cuts through the grape field en route to Makuan.

Photo courtesy of Captain Nicholas Williams

Ten minutes after the first MICLIC fired, the ABV rolled through the initial breach point, shot a second MICLIC into the sky, and again clanked forward. But when it fired a third MICLIC, the line charge failed to explode. A Marine ran out of the vehicle, attached hand-held charges and detonated it himself.[18] "That guy right there deserves a medal," said First Sergeant Stone. After the third explosion, Bravo's men moved to the ABV's flanks, providing security. "We were worried that [the enemy] would try and take *it out," explained Stone.[19] Unfortunately, the MICLIC's devastating effects made the bomb-sniffing dogs paranoid and edgy. According to Lieutenant Murphy, walking though an area blasted by a MICLIC "kind of messed up their noses because you have 2,000 pounds of explosive ordnance out there. So having them out during the initial breach is what really screwed them up for the whole operation."[20]*

The Bridge at the Canal

At 1000 Bravo Company reached a bridge over a canal running east to west across the direction of attack. Homemade explosive bags were stuffed beneath the bridge and a 10-foot pipe was buried across it. On the other side of the bridge, an IED hung from a tree. It was a clever ploy. Anyone disarming the IEDs on the bridge would expose themselves to the tree-borne IED. A waiting insurgent could detonate them both. "Anybody exposed is going to get hit by shrapnel," said Prisock. The Marines fired a MICLIC over the bridge, but the resulting explosion failed to ignite the explosives on the bridge. The EOD men explained to Prisock that they could not blow the bridge without first securing the other end. The threat of enemy attack by direct and indirect fire was simply too great.[21]

Figure 3. Two IEDs lay partially concealed on the far bank of the bridge over the canal (inside circle).

Photo courtesy of First Lieutenant Taylor Murphy

Captain Prisock called in an airstrike. Two A-10 Thunderbolt II ground-attack aircraft swooped in and dropped two 500-pound Guided Bomb Units (GBUs), destroying the bridge and detonating approximately nine IEDs. Prisock then ordered two MICLICs to fire east and west of the bridge, parallel to the canal, detonating seven IEDs and clearing out a wider avenue of approach. The Seabees began plowing mud with their D7 bulldozers, creating an impromptu bridge, but they failed to transport a collection of large steel pipes that would have served as the base for the mound, allowing water to flow through the new bridge. By 1600, with nowhere for the water to go, the area flooded. Prisock explained to the Seabees what needed to be done and oversaw their work. "It was just weird," said Lieutenant Williams, "having infantry guys telling the Seabees, whose job it is to build stuff, how to build the bridge."[22] Stalled at the bridge, Bravo Company could no longer keep driving the enemy in front of it. Replacing the bridge seriously delayed the push to Makuan.[23]

Lieutenant Ragland's 1st Platoon and Lieutenant Murphy's 2d Platoon pulled security along the canal's north bank, east and west of the bridge, respectively. Ragland deployed behind a dirt berm when one of his soldiers, Specialist Mark Baidinger, told Sergeant Nicholas Christensen he had to see the medic. Christensen agreed but told him to walk behind him and not up on the berm, where he would be exposed. "Roger, Sergeant," Baidinger said, but stepped on top of the berm anyway.[24] Suddenly, the enemy opened fire from across the canal with a B-10 82mm recoilless rifle. The round hit a tree above Baidinger, raining shrapnel and lacerating his left arm, leg and back, and breaking his femur. A piece of shrapnel caught Sergeant Derek Dodd in the neck. Several Soldiers carried Baidinger to the rear while Captain Prisock called for a medical evacuation (MEDEVAC). Sergeant Dodd stayed in the fight.[25]

The enemy then opened up with rocket propelled grenades (RPGs), machine guns, and AK47 assault rifles from behind a mud wall. Both platoons returned fire with small arms and an M240 medium machine gun. Soon 60mm and 120mm mortars, along with 155mm artillery, added to the fight. "[We] could see them moving in the wood line," explained Staff Sergeant Zac McDonald. "They weren't static." With the canal separating the enemy from the two platoons and the bridge unusable, the Americans could only return fire. "We weren't in a situation where we could chase them," McDonald added.[26] Instead of firing from cover, the untrained ANA soldiers stood up while shooting from the hip. They simply lacked the Americans' level of training and did not have enough time in the field.[27]

When Prisock's 60mm mortars ran out of ammunition, Captain Rella sent for resupply, and a Light Medium Tactical Vehicle (LMTV) sped down the dirt road to the mortar position. Soldiers threw green smoke grenades to cover the mortar crews running back to retrieve the ammo. Unfortunately, the smoke served an unintended purpose: the MEDEVAC HH-60 Black Hawk helicopter pilot, misinterpreting the smoke as a landing zone, swooped in and tried to land within range of the enemy fire. Specialist Leigh tried to raise the pilot on the radio, but could not find his frequency. He then contacted the battalion headquarters, hoping they would relay his directions to the HH-60 before it landed. First Sergeant Stone threw clods of dirt at the helicopter, trying to get the pilot's attention. Other Soldiers stopped firing, ran over to the landing helicopter, and waved it off. The helicopter then circled and tried to land again. The men repeated the process. Finally, the Black Hawk left the firefight and landed in 3d Platoon's rear perimeter. "He basically landed right on top of me," explained Staff Sergeant Joseph Jackel, who told the MEDEVAC crew chief, "Get the hell out here! We've already got the casualty up on the road."[28]

The mortars made the difference. The suppression provided by the high explosive rounds and the smoke provided by the white phosphorous rounds eventually gave the Americans fire superiority over their well-entrenched enemy. When the insurgents broke contact, Lieutenant Williams led his platoon splashing across the canal, where they found a big mud wall from where the enemy had fired. Holes were dug under the wall for hideouts and weapons storage. Bravo Company encountered more of these mud walls throughout the operation. "The area where we were was almost built for trench warfare," explained Lieutenant Charles Ragland.[9]

Makuan

After the initial confrontation, the company cleared the final 200 meters south into Makuan. With the sun setting, Lieutenant Williams wanted to move quickly, but refused to rush his men in an IED-infested area. In the darkness, the men secured two compounds on the town's northeast corner, designated Strong Point One and Strong Point Two. Bravo Company's Headquarters and 1st and 2d platoons occupied Strong Point One, while 3d Platoon and most of the ANA occupied Strong Point Two. Using white lights attached to their rifles and mine detectors, the men cleared the buildings. "If we saw something," explained Lieutenant Williams, "we tied 550 [cord] to it, we backed out of the room and we'd pull it in case it was some kind of tamper."[30] For security, Lieutenant Murphy's mortar crews emplaced their weapons and fired off a few illumination rounds to set their base plates into the ground. During this part of the operation, the men of Bravo Company encountered no one.[31]

The exhausted men finished clearing the strong points by 0130 the next morning. Some Soldiers set up security positions while others bedded down. Unfortunately, everyone's assault packs were north of the canal, leaving the men to curl up on the floor without their blankets or cold-weather gear as the temperature dropped. Many Soldiers were still wet from the canal crossing. Making matters worse, Army engineers began blowing up a nearby tree line to provide better fields of fire and deprive the enemy of cover and concealment. The engineers attached blocks of C4 to the trees and ignited the fuses.[32] Some white phosphorous from the day's battle set off one of the fuses early. An engineer smelled the burning fuse and told everyone to get inside the compound, which they did as the charge detonated. "No one was injured," said Murphy, "but that was a close call."[33]

The engineers' work proved dangerous for Bravo's men. Lieutenant Ragland was talking to one of his team leaders inside Strong Point One when an explosion erupted outside. "A huge fireball comes in the room," recalled Ragland. "We thought we were getting attacked."[34] Other nearby detonations lifted sleeping men off the floor and slammed them back down. Sergeant Christensen was sleeping in a sheep hut when a huge explosion woke him. He thought an RPG had hit. Grabbing his rifle, he escaped as the roof caved in. Once out, he ran into Prisock, who asked "Are you okay?"[35] He was, but the engineers continued their work until daylight, making sleep difficult for the men.[36]

First Day in Makuan

By 0300 that morning, the tired Soldiers of Bravo Company began clearing Makuan. Lieutenants Murphy and Williams' platoons cleared compounds, while Ragland's 1st Platoon leveled the trees lines along the wadis. With all their heavy support vehicles north of the canal, the men used C4 explosives to blow holes in mud walls surrounding pomegranate orchards and fired anti-personnel obstacle breaching systems (APOBs), a smaller two-man version of the MICLIC, to clear paths along trails and roads. IEDs infested the area. Whenever the Soldiers fired an APOB, there were numerous sympathetic detonations. The men even found two IEDs just outside Strong Point Two.[37]

Inside Makuan's various buildings, the men found cartons and wrappers for 82mm recoilless rifle boosters, RPG rounds, and other Soviet-era ammunition. They also discovered parts of land mines. The buildings contained fresh fruits and vegetables and plenty of bedding but no personal items.³⁸ It was, according to Lieutenant Murphy, "just a bed-down location."³⁹ All of the compounds were empty, but the men knew Makuan was no ghost town. "We pretty much had that feeling most of the time that they were watching us," explained Specialist Leigh, "that there was somebody out there."⁴⁰

The enemy had not abandoned the area. Providing security for engineers blowing up trees, Lieutenant Murphy's 2d platoon deployed along a chest-high wall across from a pomegranate orchard. Suddenly, an enemy recoilless rifle round exploded against the wall. Specialist Christopher Tolintino, although protected by the wall, was caught in the blast. He stumbled backwards and doubled over. Murphy ran over to him, but Tolintino was okay. "He got his bell rung pretty good," remembered Specialist Leigh.⁴¹

The platoon fired into the pomegranate orchard but the shooter did not return fire. Approximately a half-hour later, the enemy opened up again, this time with AK47s. Lieutenant Murphy's men spotted two individuals running through the orchard and opened fire. "They were running pretty fast," said Murphy, "and if we did hit them, it didn't slow them down." Murphy called in mortars, and while adjusting fire, another recoilless rifle round exploded in the distance, followed by accurate PKM machine-gun fire.⁴² "I never felt machine-gun fire in that amount of mass before," explained Sergeant Zac McDonald. "It was a massive roar…and they had to have multiple PKMs in multiple positions to be able to match that fire."⁴³

Murphy stood behind the wall, holding his M4 rifle against his chest with his right hand when he felt something impact on his chest plate. He reflexively stuck his hand under the plate to see if he had been hit. Seeing no blood, he continued to call in rounds and fire his rifle. As rounds smacked around Murphy's head, he had his machine gunner set up a firing position at a gap in the wall, then reported the situation to Prisock, and called in aerial support fire from the on-station AH-64 Apache and OH-58 Kiowa helicopters. Staff Sergeant McDonald asked Murphy if he was okay and began checking his body when he noticed blood dripping from Murphy's right glove. Murphy had, in fact, been hit in the wrist. McDonald applied a tourniquet to Murphy's arm as a precaution.⁴⁴ When Staff Sergeant Jaime Newman heard what happened, he brought up the medic, Specialist Michael Babinski, who loosened the tourniquet and wrapped a Kerlix bandage on the wound.⁴⁵ Everyone kept telling Murphy to get his wrist examined, but he just brushed them off. "I'm good, I'm good," he insisted.⁴⁶

Two Delta Company MRAP All Terrain Vehicles (M-ATVs), which had crossed the now-completed bridge, added to Murphy's return fire with Mark 19 grenade launchers and .50-caliber machine guns, but, in the confusion, also fired at Williams' 3d Platoon on Murphy's right flank. Captain Prisock called the Delta Company commander and told him to cease fire. It took two tries before the Delta Company men stopped firing. Prisock's Air Force Joint Terminal Attack Controllers (JTAC) directed helicopter gunships firing 2.75mm rockets and 30mm cannons at selected targets. Then Prisock brought his 60mm mortar men forward, who fired all their rounds in hand-held mode. Prisock added A-10s to the collective effort, which flew gun runs along the pomegranate field and dropped bombs, flushing out the enemy.[47]

While Lieutenant Murphy coordinated fire suppression on the northern section of the orchard, Lieutenant Williams maneuvered his 3d Platoon to the west side of the orchard. While Williams' men prepared to breach a compound wall, a recoilless rifle round slammed into the compound. The Soldiers took cover. A-10s bombed the orchard, and Williams' men breached the wall and entered the compound. They climbed onto the roof where they exchanged fire with insurgents in a wadi line until Staff Sergeant Heneghan shouted, "Cease fire! Cease fire!"[48]

An insurgent fired at Williams' men and ran into the pomegranate orchard. The men opened fire but failed to hit him.[49] *An Apache helicopter pursued, firing its 30mm chain gun. The A-10s spotted another insurgent in a wadi line 400 meters from William's men and strafed the area. "We saw part of his torso fly through the air," recalled Williams.*[50] *The JTACs continued to guide A-10s bombing missions on enemy strong points. Prisock followed up the airstrikes with 120mm mortars. All the while, Williams' platoon remained in the compound, providing overwatch for Murphy. "It was one of the more intense firefights I've been in," explained Staff Sergeant Joshua Reese, one of Williams' squad leaders.*[51]

With the enemy suppressed, Lieutenant Murphy led his platoon into the pomegranate orchard, using APOBs to clear a path. They found empty enemy firing positions, brass casings, and a bloodstain on the ground. Murphy led his men further south, looking for insurgents and conducting a bomb damage assessment (BDA) on a compound levelled by a 500-pound bomb. As night fell, the Soldiers, not finding anything, returned to Strong Point One.[52]

In the dark, a sergeant from Lieutenant Williams' platoon spotted two insurgents, and instead of firing at them, asked Williams what he should do.

By the time Williams said "engage," the two took off running toward two structures. Captain Prisock called the A-10s to bomb the structures. The bombing required a BDA, so Williams led his men, in the dark, to the area where they found evidence of one bomb, but not the other. "You'd think it would be easy to find a 500-pound bomb drop," explained Williams, "but it went right through the ceiling and no debris had come into the clearing, so we really can't find it."[53]

Figure 4. A Bravo Company Soldier conducts a bomb damage assessment on a Makuan compound.

Photo courtesy of Captain Nicholas Williams

As the men prepared to bed down for the night, some could hear the enemy reoccupying the village and digging holes for more IEDs. "You knew they were out there," explained First Sergeant Stone.[54] *Staff Sergeant Reese admitted, "It was a really sickening feeling. I personally heard them digging." Captain Prisock could hear prayers from a nearby mosque.*[55]

Captain Prisock met with Lieutenant Colonel Johnny Davis, the battalion commander, and explained the futility of checking every empty compound in an area that included, according to Prisock, "tons of IEDs." The results were not worth the effort, or, as Captain Prisock told Davis, "The juice is not worth the squeeze."[56] *Davis agreed, but pointed out the battalion's limited window on its ABVs and air assets to complete DRAGON STRIKE. He expressed confidence that Prisock had enough* support elements to clear Makuan. "Brandon, I think you can do it," said Davis. "I think we can clear this and get to the next wadi line, so that we can cut this facilitation zone in half because remember, we're just one part of the Dragon Strike."[57] The two officers agreed to build up the strong points, destroy the tree lines, clear the trails around the strong points and improve the bridge and roads. The ultimate goal became creating a combat outpost in Makuan and preventing the enemy from returning.[58]

Around midnight, Lieutenant Murphy finally had a chance to take off his body armor. He found a bullet lodged in it. "I was pretty pissed off because it had actually shattered my camera." He brought his armor plate to the ANP station and switched it with a new one. An ANP officer pried the bullet out of Murphy's chest plate and explained he needed to keep the bullet for forensic evidence. Murphy would have no souvenir.[59]

Second Day in Makuan

Before sunrise on 16 September, Bravo's three platoons headed out once again, searching for IEDs and clearing tree lines. They engaged the enemy twice during the day: first, against a lone teenager with an AK47 who fled at the sight of the Americans; second, when insurgents fired at some Delta Company trucks. In both cases, the Soldiers opened fire with small arms and called for fire support from orbiting A-10s.[60]

That night, around 1930, orders came down from battalion that Lieutenant Colonel Davis needed Makuan entirely cleared by 1200 the next day. Davis wanted Bravo Company to push down to a wadi line south of the town, enabling his other companies to continue their operations on Bravo's flanks. To meet this deadline, Prisock needed to send his Soldiers out at night, the most dangerous time to search for IEDs.[61] "He was kind of between a rock and a hard place," explained Specialist Leigh. "Everybody knew that doing this at night was a bad idea."[62] The company had already come across numerous IEDs. "The town was rigged," said Captain Rella, the XO, "it's got nothing but anti-personnel mines all over the place and [IEDs in buildings]."[63] Staff Sergeant Jackel was more blunt, "You don't patrol at night because of the IED threat. You can't see [anything]."[64]

As the sun set, Lieutenant Williams led 15 Americans, six ANA Soldiers, and a bomb-sniffing German Shepherd named Blek, out of Strong Point One. All of the men wore night vision goggles (NVGs). In the town, the Soldiers climbed to the roof of a compound where they had conducted the previous night's BDA and worked their way down into the rooms, finding bomb-making materials. Some of Williams' men returned to the compound where they had provided overwatch for Lieutenant Murphy the day before and set up security posts on the roof, while Williams and the rest of the men searched a nearby two-story grape hut.[65]

The ANA soldiers refused to walk up the grape hut's exterior stairs, so an American swept the stairs with a mine detector. Air Force Staff Sergeant Brent Olson sent Blek sniffing up and down the stairs. Convinced that the stairs were safe, the ANA soldiers headed up. The first Soldier made it up the stairs, but as the second reached the third step, he triggered an IED. There was a flash, and smoke blinded everyone. The ANA Soldier's legs were nearly blown off. He screamed in pain, joined by others who had been hit by shrapnel. Staff Sergeant Jackel shouted "IED! IED!" as Staff Sergeant Heneghan rolled on the ground, shouting that he could not hear anything. Other Soldiers fell wounded. Staff Sergeant Olson stumbled around the base of the stairs as Blek whimpered from shrapnel wounds.[66]

Staff Sergeant Olson reeled in Blek's leash and checked him for wounds. "While I was doing that," recalled Olson, "I felt my right arm start to go numb and it just fell." He felt under his right armpit with his left hand and found blood. "I'm hit," he called out. In the smoke and confusion, others shouted back "Who's hit?" "The dog handler!" Olson replied. He dropped to a knee and was falling backwards when the platoon medic caught him. Olson suffered a broken right arm, a burn on his left arm, a piece of metal sticking out of his leg above the knee, and shrapnel wounds throughout his upper body.[67] Lieutenant Williams flipped up his NVGs and turned on the blue light attached to his rifle, looking for blood on the ground and on his soldiers. Other men turned on their white lights. Staff Sergeant Jackel ordered the uninjured men to stand still, face out, and pull security. "Don't move!" he yelled, not wanting to set off another IED.[68]

Back at Strong Point One, the Soldiers, hearing the explosion, donned their gear and put on their NVGs. Staff Sergeant Newman told Staff Sergeant Roberts to organize a fire team and set up a helicopter landing zone (HLZ) for Williams' position. As Roberts led his team out the door, Sergeant McDonald rushed over to Lieutenant Murphy and told him his men were ready. "Stand by," explained Murphy, "let's see what happens."[69]

At the blast site, Lieutenant Williams dragged the injured ANA Soldier to a casualty collection point (CCP) in the compound where his men stood overwatch. "I could see his femur sticking out," said Williams, "and his other leg is real mangled." But when Williams reached the compound's wall, he found fresh IEDs inside. "I guess they had seen us earlier and had to infil behind us from a back door once we left," said Williams. "[We] either interrupted them or they didn't have time [to arm the IEDs]." As

Williams sought a new place to bring the ANA Soldier, three other ANA Soldiers came running up the road to him. "I'm trying to tell them to stop," said Williams, not wanting people to move around excessively. Just then, one of the ANA Soldiers stepped on an IED five feet from Williams. [70]

Williams found himself on the ground with his ears ringing. He felt nauseous. He got up and checked the ANA soldiers. One was fine, one had lost a leg, and the third had lost both legs below the knees. Williams began placing tourniquets on the men's arms and legs. "I think I used six tourniquets," he said. Staff Sergeant Heneghan, already injured in the first blast, was sitting nearby when the second IED detonated. "After the second one, he was done," explained Williams. "He literally was lying on the ground yelling at people." Williams set up a new CCP about ten meters away in another compound's courtyard and moved Heneghan there, bleeding from the ears.[71] *Several Soldiers helped Staff Sergeant Olson walk to the CCP. Olson refused to be placed on a poleless litter. "There's no support structure," Olson said of the flimsy device that relied on straps instead of poles. But Olson's condition worsened. Feeling light headed, he asked his comrades to help him get down on his knees. He called to Blek and started petting him. "[Blek] didn't even realize I was there," Olson recalled.*[72]

Williams assessed his situation. Altogether, he had 11 casualties on his hands: seven Americans, three ANA, and one dog. Two men were urgent surgical: the ANA Soldier who stepped on the first IED and Staff Sergeant Olson, who was bleeding profusely. In a span of five minutes, two IEDs had cut Williams' unit strength in half. He realized the enemy had lined the whole road with IEDs. The uninjured ANA Soldiers panicked. Screaming and yelling, they pointed their M16 rifles at the Americans. Williams' translator forgot every word of English he knew and sat on the ground. The ANA soldiers picked up their wounded comrades and carried them back to Strong Point One.[73]

Lieutenant Murphy's Reaction Force

Back at Strong Point One, everyone heard the second explosion. They listened as Staff Sergeant Jackel reported, "I need help, I've got more casualties than I can secure or move."[74] *The ANA at the strong points were anxious. They demanded permission to leave but Captain Prisock did not want them going outside. "The ANA were relatively untrained, [had] very poor discipline [and] no night vision devices," he explained.*[75] *First Sergeant Stone was able to calm the ANA at Strong Point One but at Strong Point Two the ANA were more forceful. When Staff Sergeant*

Joshua Reese blocked the door, ANA Soldiers pointed their M16s at him. He let them leave. As the ANA ran out in a disorganized manner, one fired into the air, sending tracers over the heads of Lieutenant Williams and his men. "That put everyone on edge," said Williams.[76] Seeing the tracers and the unidentified ANA soldiers rushing around, Jackel called back to Strong Point One, "I think we're going to get overrun."[77]

Captain Prisock contacted Battalion Headquarters and reported that he had a mass casualty situation (MASCAL) alerting the MEDEVACs. He told Lieutenant Murphy to get down to Lieutenant Williams' position and help set up an HLZ. Murphy ran outside and told Sergeant Roberts that he now needed his whole squad as a reaction force to head towards Williams.[78] Everyone wanted to head out. Sergeant Christensen organized his squad until First Sergeant Stone told him to recharge his hand-held IED jammers.[79] As Christensen changed his batteries, Staff Sergeant Newman approached him and said, "Hey, man, I've got a set that works right now, my guys are ready to go. Let me take this." Christensen agreed and told him, "All right brother, I'll be right behind you, as soon as they let me go."[80]

Lieutenant Murphy, now with a whole squad, reviewed the route with Sergeant McDonald, who led the unit. Captain Prisock had planned to go out with Murphy, but was delayed as Lieutenant Eric Yates, the Fire Support Officer, prepared his gear. Murphy led his force out to Williams' position, soon followed by Prisock and a handful of his headquarters Soldiers. As Prisock's team crossed through a marijuana field, they noticed an ANA Soldier pass by with a wounded comrade on his back, headed to Strong Point One.[81]

The two ANA soldiers approached the front gate where Sergeant Scot Gerwitz stood guard. Gerwitz tried to help them but one pointed his M16 rifle in Gerwitz's face. Gerwitz grabbed the weapon, tossed it aside and helped the injured ANA Soldier to Strong Point One's CCP, which First Sergeant Stone had established, along with a second HLZ. Lieutenant Ragland's men laid out infrared chemical lights to guide the helicopters. When the first Black Hawk landed, the men loaded the ANA soldiers with missing legs. Trucks from the ANA and Delta Company also arrived to take more wounded north. As more ANA Soldiers drifted into the strong points, the men inside ripped up shirts for bandages and broke up a ladder to create splints. When they ran out of tourniquets, the men fashioned their own.[82]

Lieutenant Murphy's team continued south toward Williams. When Murphy told Sergeant McDonald to push forward, Staff Sergeant Newman preached caution, "Lieutenant, would you think about this a little bit and make sure we're doing the right thing?" Murphy took his advice, stopped, and sent McDonald to find the best way to Williams. McDonald pushed through a marijuana field and made contact with a few of Williams' men. "They were spread real thin because they had been hit with those IEDs," said McDonald, who reported back to Murphy that the link was established.[83]

Meanwhile, Captain Prisock's team made it through the marijuana field and caught up with Murphy's men on a trail along a wall. In the darkness, Lieutenant Yates, following behind Sergeant Newman and Prisock, stepped on another IED. The powerful blast knocked everyone down. Debris flew through the air, peppering the soldiers. The heat was intense. "It felt like all of a sudden somebody opened an oven right behind you," said Prisock who dropped to one knee as something large flew by his right side.[84] Specialist Babinski, the medic, was thrown up against a wall. Screams again filled the air. Weapons and equipment littered the ground.[85]

In the blinding dust, Sergeant McDonald grabbed Lieutenant Murphy and asked him if he was okay. "I'm all right, I'm all right," Murphy replied. Both had been hit in the back with shrapnel.[86] Everyone who could flipped up their NVGs and turned on their red, white, or blue lights. "The threat of casualties bleeding out overwhelmed our fear of the enemy seeing our lights," explained Murphy. "They already knew where we were anyway."[87] Murphy and McDonald assessed the casualties, trying to find out the severity of the injuries and figure out who was healthy enough to pull security. Murphy found Yates first, mortally wounded but conscious. He reassured Yates that he was going to be okay. "Yeah," said Yates, "I'll be okay. I know you got me."[88] Soldiers moved Yates into the blast hole—the safest place after an IED attack. Specialist Babinski shook Yates. He did not respond. Babinski asked for some light so he could assess Yates wounds. Other soldiers were shouting "Medic!" so he instructed the men around Yates to apply tourniquets while he assessed the other casualties.[89]

Babinski checked everyone near the blast site. Some were cut from shrapnel, others from rocks. Most were dazed. "Luckily, they were in the prone [position] so they didn't catch [much] shrapnel," explained Babinski. Pieces of shrapnel lodged above Sergeant Roberts' Adam's apple and his cheek.[90] Babinski returned to Yates, checked the tourniquets and stuffed combat gauze into his wounds. Yates opened his eyes and asked Babinski how he was doing. "Pretty good," Babinski replied and asked Yates how he was feeling. "Tired," was his only reply as he closed his eyes.[91] Captain Prisock showed up and told Yates, "Hey, stick with us, hang in there, stay with us." Yates opened his eyes again. "Hey, I'm with you," said Prisock. The two men then said a prayer together.[92]

Lieutenant Murphy told Prisock he had 12 wounded and only five or six combat-effective Soldiers. Prisock raised Lieutenant Colonel Davis on the radio and told him he had a second MASCAL and needed multiple MEDEVACs.[93] Now there would be three HLZs: one for Williams' 3d Platoon, one for Murphy's 2d, and one for the strong points. First Sergeant Stone organized all three from Strong Point One and coordinated the MEDEVACs. Staff Sergeant Christensen, watching Stone's actions, was impressed with how smoothly he ran the three MASCALS. "He did an outstanding job," Christensen recalled.[94]

Lieutenant Murphy established security while Sergeant McDonald set up a CCP in the middle of the marijuana field. Those uninjured helped the wounded and set up an HLZ in a wheat field on the edge of the marijuana rows. Murphy and several men carried Lieutenant Yates on a poleless litter, but he kept sliding off in the rough terrain and the men kept stopping or slowing down to put him back on. Soldiers took turns holding his hand as they brought him to the CCP. While they waited for the helicopters, Murphy made his way to 3d platoon's area, found Lieutenant Williams and told him there was no way 2d Platoon could assist him. Williams said his men were capable of evacuating their own wounded. Murphy then asked Williams if he had seen Staff Sergeant Newman, saying "I can't find him." Williams said he had not. His mission completed, Murphy returned to his platoon.[95]

Approximately seven MEDEVAC helicopters circled above Makuan. At Lieutenant Williams' position, Williams and Staff Sergeant Jackel spun chemical lights on strings, making a glowing propeller called a "buzz saw." The pilots were taking things slow, not risking a mid-air collision by coming in too fast. At Lieutenant Murphy's position, the first helicopter landed and the men rushed Lieutenant Yates to it. Specialist Babinski briefed the flight medic on Yates' condition. As the Bravo men gathered other casualties, the flight medic jumped back into the helicopter as it took off. Yates was an emergency case and the crew wanted to get him to help quickly. When Prisock had difficulty contacting other Army MEDEVACs, his JTACs called in Air Force Pararescue Jumper helicopters. They landed at both Murphy and Williams' positions and loaded the wounded Americans but the ANA were nowhere to be found. They had all left on foot.[96]

At Lieutenant Murphy's location, the men had finished loading the last wounded when Specialist Babinski brought Murphy a list of names of those *evacuated. Staff Sergeant Newman's name was not on the list. Someone suggested that Newman had walked back to the strong points. Sergeant McDonald could not raise Newman on the radio. "My initial worry was that he was hurt, couldn't defend himself, and [the enemy was] a lot closer to us than we imagined," he said.[97] The rest of the men returned to the blast site, seeking to avoid IEDs. They found Newman's ID card, pieces of his uniform, and his ammo pouch in a tree. They noticed a bloodstain on the mud wall about 20 meters from the blast site.[98]*

While Sergeant McDonald checked the other side of the wall, Lieutenant Murphy discovered Newman's body in a ditch. They deduced that the blast threw Newman backward into the wall, before he rolled forward into the ditch. It was Newman who flew past Captain Prisock's right side at the moment of the explosion.[99] The men put Newman into a body bag and placed it onto a litter. Four men, including Murphy, picked up the litter and carried it back to Strong Point One until Murphy asked the men if he could change hands, since he was holding the litter handle with his wounded hand. "We kind of felt like idiots for not remembering his wrist was all messed up," recalled Specialist Babinski. "But he didn't stop at all. He kept going."[100]

During the search for Staff Sergeant Newman, Specialist Leigh became disoriented and dropped to a knee. He also had trouble breathing. As the men carried Newman's body back to Strong Point One, Leigh vomited. He told Captain Prisock he felt fine, trying to reassure his commander that he had not suffered a concussion, but his words were disjointed and confused. He vomited again.[101] Other soldiers were doing the same, suffering the delayed effects of over-pressure sickness and traumatic brain injury (TBI). Soldiers from 1st Platoon arrived from Strong Point Two and brought the men all the way back to the canal bridge where they rendezvoused with an MRAP to bring them to the ANP station for treatment.[102] As Leigh climbed into the MRAP, he turned to Captain Rella, "Well, at least I'm going to get my Purple Heart, Sir." Rella agreed.[103] In all, 26 American and ANA soldiers were evacuated that night.[104]

First Sergeant Stone conducted an equipment check on all the Soldiers and discovered that Lieutenant Yates' Advanced Special Improvement Program (ASIP) radio was missing. Soldiers from Lieutenant Ragland's 1st Platoon relieved Murphy's 2d Platoon and searched for the radio, which could not be allowed to fall into enemy hands. After searching around the blast area, Ragland called for the engineers, who used APOBs to blast paths through the fields or knock down walls. "[We] saw the blood all over," said Lieutenant Ragland, "but [we] couldn't really find anything to bring back."[105] After almost an hour-long search, Captain Prisock decided the mission was not worth the risk and ordered the men to return.[106]

Lieutenant Williams and the rest of his men finally arrived at Strong Point One after taking a circuitous route, making sure not to follow the same path they used on the way out. Everyone was checked for signs of hearing loss and TBI. Some were evacuated by trucks. Sergeant Gerwitz, now Lieutenant Murphy's acting platoon sergeant, told his returning men to go sit by the fire. "Try to get warm," he told them, "try to get some rest."[107] Many men suffered from headaches and swollen limbs. Then word then reached the men that Yates had died. "They were shaken up," said Lieutenant Ragland.[108] Some of the men removed equipment off Sergeant Newman's body in preparation for the trip to the ANP station. The last piece they lifted was a document in several Afghan languages which began, "I am an American Soldier."[109]

Captain Prisock radioed Lieutenant Colonel Davis and the two officers agreed to bomb the area where Lieutenant Yates lost his radio. Now convinced that Makuan held no civilians, Davis changed the mission from clearing the town for an outpost to eliminating the settlement. They planned to hit the area with Guided-Multiple Launch Rocket System (G-MLRS) artillery. If Yates' radio was still in the area, the G-MLRS would blast it to bits, along with any insurgents and IEDs.[110]

The next morning at sunrise, most of the men retreated into the strong points as 40 to 50 G-MLRS rockets flew over and exploded in the IED blast area. Prisock described the rockets flying overhead as "black telephone poles, just descending."[111] "Everything was rock, rattle and shake," said Staff Sergeant Roberts.[112] "It was pretty phenomenal," added Lieutenant Murphy.[113] Lieutenant Williams did not think so. The explosions woke him out of a dead sleep. "I'm scrambling," said Williams, "I'm trying to grab my M4, my helmet, and I'm like 'What's going on? Not again!'" The explosion lifted the men's spirits after a difficult operation. "It made their hearts happy," said Staff Sergeant Roberts. "[It] made them feel better to have some sort of retaliation."[114]

Within days, Bravo Company departed the area. Other elements of 1st Battalion, 502d IN moved in and leveled the remaining structures and destroyed additional tree lines. By the time they were done, they had, according to Staff Sergeant Jackel, "turned it into a parking lot."[115] When Sergeant McDonald returned to the town almost a week later with Alpha Company, he did not recognize the area. "From the time that I first saw it to when it was completely finished was pretty much night and day," said McDonald. "There was nothing there.[116] Makuan eventually became a combat outpost and never again supported enemy operations as a bed-down area, a bomb-producing facility, or a consolidation area for ambushes on Highway One. An objective of DRAGON STRIKE had been accomplished, but Bravo Company paid a heavy price to deprive Makuan from the enemy.[117]

Conclusion

Bravo Company overcame numerous obstacles to return Makuan to government control. The Soldiers used their training and assets to clear IEDs, destroy fighting positions, and eliminate IED-making facilities. "The threat was killing not only us, but the ANA, the ANP, and the local civilians," explained Lieutenant Colonel Davis. When the operation ended, local farmers returned to the area south of Highway One and thanked the Soldiers, telling them "this area has been the Taliban's area, we just wanted to be farmers again."[118]

The Makuan operation also proved the utility of joint operations. The Marine Corps breached the IED belts south of Highway One. Navy Seabees worked on the front line to build (and rebuild) the bridge over the canal and Navy bomb-sniffing dogs added to the company's capability. The Air Force provided combat air support, pararescue helicopters, JTACs, as well as bomb-sniffing dogs. Throughout the operation, the services collectively coordinated their efforts for the best possible result. Captain Prisock praised the joint effort, "Soldiers, Marines, Airmen, and Sailors alike constantly faced and overcame great danger, maintaining their composure and commitment to both the mission and one another," he explained.[119] Advanced weapons systems, such as MICLIC-firing ABVs and APOBs, also gave the Americans a distinct advantage over the enemy embedded in a safe haven that dated back to the Soviet-Afghan War.

Captain Prisock considered the destruction of the bridge on 15 September the key to the operation. If Bravo had kept the bridge intact, or had a portable bridge readily available, they would have been able to advance south faster, bringing in MRAPs and other heavy vehicles, and quickly push all the way down to the Arghandab River. They also would have had more daylight to identify and remove IEDs. As it was, Bravo ended up stalled at the bridge on the first day, giving the enemy time to recover and attack Lieutenant Ragland's 1st Platoon, inflicting casualties.

Some of Bravo Company's assets did not achieve the expected results. Most of the men grew distrustful of their bomb-sniffing dogs, feeling they only provided a false sense of security. The dogs got off to a poor start when the MICLICs first breached the enemy line.[120] First Sergeant Stone explained that the dogs panicked every time an explosive detonated, adding "nobody really trusted them."[121] Lieutenant Williams thought both the dogs and their trainers were very professional, but the dogs could not handle the Afghan heat. The dog handlers would often tell him "He's done, he's not going to be very effective anymore."[122] Staff Sergeant Roberts saw some benefit, "I'm not going to walk out there without a dog if the dog is available."[123] While the dogs had been trained to detect odors specific to IEDs, the enemy often masked those odors. In addition, the dog handlers found it difficult to read their dogs at night while wearing NVGs. This might explain why Blek failed to detect the IED in the staircase. Staff Sergeant Olson stressed that "there's no odor in a pressure plate," adding "I can't say that I really saw anything in my dog that could have prevented it."[124]

Other factors proved a challenge to the Soldiers. Almost everyone in the company admitted how exhausted they were when DRAGON STRIKE kicked off, and they caught little sleep on the following days. "We had already been up for two days [prior to DRAGON STRIKE]," explained First Sergeant Stone.[125] "We were so run down, and just barely making it," recalled Staff Sergeant Christensen.[126] Specialist Leigh remembered that exhaustion tested everyone. "We were running on no sleep, and bad food, and it tested the Soldiers probably more than [anything else]."[127] Most men stressed they were more fatigued on this operation than any other time in their military careers.[128]

Bravo Company's officers and NCOs agreed that going into a built-up area at night invited trouble. "We had seen the IEDs," said Staff Sergeant Roberts, explaining that the enemy had already placed IEDs all over Makuan before they pulled out. "They go back and hook up the batteries before you come, so when you come through there, it's hot, and at nighttime, you can't see anything."[129] Staff Sergeant Jackel called operations at night misguided. "That was one of my platoon's tactics, techniques, and procedures. We don't patrol at night," he said.[130] Lieutenant Williams felt that it was easiest to spot IEDs visually, in daylight, where anything that looked odd usually revealed an IED. "[The enemy] kicks some rocks over [the IEDs] or a rock with a wire sticking out, because they know they don't have all day to do it, so they got to rush."[131] First Sergeant Stone defended the night maneuver, despite the heavy IED infestation, "From a tactical viewpoint we knew that if we were going to catch them bedded down, the best time to do that was at night."[132]

Also, by operating during the day and returning to the strong points at night, the company allowed the enemy to reoccupy compounds previously cleared. The air assault originally planned for Makuan would have solved this problem by trapping the enemy between two forces. When Bravo instead attacked on the ground, the enemy was able to retreat and return. Staff Sergeant Heneghan explained the unit's frustration about revisiting areas already cleared the previous day. "We had already been down there ... and they wanted us to go back down there again at this time, at night."[133]

Bravo Company did have the benefit of excellent leadership. Captain Prisock commanded Bravo Company for only 10 days prior to DRAGON STRIKE, but he led from the front and shared his men's burdens. He called in the A-10s to destroy the bridge over the canal, brought support fire when Lieutenant Murphy engaged the enemy, and went out with Murphy's unit when the ANA Soldier stepped on the IED. He also made sure his men knew how to use any asset available to them, from fire support to heavy weapons. "We had the assets at the time and he wanted to make sure the soldiers knew how to employ those assets," explained First Sergeant Stone.[134] "That decision to place Brandon in [command of Bravo Company] was certainly the right decision," said Lieutenant Colonel Davis, "and he really... did well, Brandon Prisock took it to the next level." Prisock's lieutenants and NCOs also performed their duties despite wounds, little sleep, and a tenacious enemy.[135]

Despite the hardships and delays, Bravo Company performed professionally and bravely, clearing IEDs and engaging the enemy. When Lieutenant Murphy and Sergeant Dodd were wounded, they stayed in the fight. During the subsequent battle, the men managed to reroute a MEDEVAC helicopter from inadvertently landing on the battlefield. During the first IED incident, every Soldier wanted to leave the strong points and help their comrades, and when the ANA panicked, the American Soldiers kept their composure and followed procedures. And despite the confusion of three IED blasts, First Sergeant Stone orchestrated three MASCALs and evacuated 26 casualties out of the area.

In clearing Makuan, the company suffered heavy casualties. Men were killed, others received severe wounds and even more suffered TBI. Yet they pressed on after the delay at the bridge and again following the firefights at the canal and Makuan. After the three IED explosions, they evacuated the wounded and searched for Lieutenant Yates' missing equipment. Prisock was proud of his men. "Without fail, everyone gave 100 percent," he said. "Their efforts and sacrifice counted."[136]

Notes

1. Carl Forsberg, "Counterinsurgency in Kandahar: Evaluating the 2010 Hamkari Campaign" Institute for the Study of War, December 2010, Afghanistan Reports, 25, 26.

2. Captain James Prisock, interview by Kevin Hymel, Combat Studies Institute, Fort Leavenworth, KS, 14 October 2011, 14.

3. Prisock, interview, 4, 5, 7, 87; Lieutenant Colonel Johnny Davis, interview by Kevin Hymel, Combat Studies Institute, Fort Leavenworth, KS, 11 December 2011, 25, 26.

4. Specialist Nicholas Leigh, interview by Kevin Hymel, Combat Studies Institute, Fort Leavenworth, KS, 26 October 2011, 2, 3.

5. Captain Luke Rella, interview by Kevin Hymel, Combat Studies Institute, Fort Leavenworth, KS, 16 November 2011, 6.

6. Prisock, interview, 9, 10, 11; Ali Ahmad and Lester W. Grau, *The Other Side of the Mountain: Mujahideen Tactics in the Soviet-Afghan War* (Princeton: Princeton University Press, 2010), 42-48.

7. Prisock, interview, 26, 27.

8. Davis, interview, 25.

9. Lieutenant Taylor Murphy, interview by Kevin Hymel, Combat Studies Institute, Fort Leavenworth, KS, 19 October 2011, 5, 6; First Sergeant Nathan Stone, interview by Kevin Hymel, Combat Studies Institute, Fort Leavenworth, KS, 8 November 2011, 4.

10. Stone, interview, 5.

11. Captain Nicholas Williams, interview by Kevin Hymel, Combat Studies Institute, Fort Leavenworth, KS, 25 October 2011, 7.

12. Staff Sergeant Nicholas Christensen, interview by Kevin Hymel, Combat Studies Institute, Fort Leavenworth, KS, 2 November 2011, 10; Davis, interview, 26; Stone, interview, 6.

13. Sergeant Zac McDonald, interview by Kevin Hymel, Combat Studies Institute, Fort Leavenworth, KS, 24 October 2011, 6.

14. Staff Sergeant Brent Olson, interview by Kevin Hymel, Combat Studies Institute, Fort Leavenworth, KS, 27 October 2011, 6.

15. Christensen, interview 11.

16. Staff Sergeant Joseph Roberts, interview by Kevin Hymel, Combat Studies Institute, Fort Leavenworth, KS, 2 November 2011, 7.

17. Prisock, interview, 12; Lieutenant Charles Ragland, interview by Kevin Hymel, Combat Studies Institute, Fort Leavenworth, KS, 31 October 2011, 17; Murphy, interview, 13.

18. John Hoellward, "ABV to Protect Combat Engineers," *Marine Corps Times*, 9 June 2007, http://www.marinecorpstimes.com/news/2007/06/marine_engineer_vehicle_070609/, accessed 10 December 2011; Prisock, interview, 20.

19. Stone, interview, 9.

20. Murphy, interview, 7, 8, 30.

21. Prisock, interview, 17, 18.

22. Williams, interview, 21.

23. Prisock, interview, 21, 28.

24. Christensen, interview, 14.

25. Staff Sergeant Ryan Heneghan, interview by Kevin Hymel, Combat Studies Institute, Fort Leavenworth, KS, 25 October 2011, 18; Stone, interview, 14.

26. McDonald, interview, 13.

27. Sergeant Scott Gerwitz, interview by Kevin Hymel, Combat Studies Institute, Fort Leavenworth, KS, 4 November 2011, 10; Prisock, interview, 40, 41.

28. Prisock, interview, 37, 40, 41; Rella, interview, 16; Leigh, interview, 13; Sergeant Joseph Jackel by interview, Kevin Hymel, Combat Studies Institute, Fort Leavenworth, KS, 25 October 2011, 10; Stone, interview, 12.

29. Ragland, interview, 25; Staff Sergeant Joshua Reese interview by Kevin Hymel, Combat Studies Institute, Fort Leavenworth, KS, 28 October 2011, 9.

30. Williams, interview, 19, 20, 22, 23.

31. Murphy, interview, 21.

32. Leigh, interview, 16, 17; Olson, interview, 10; Gerwitz, interview, 17, 18.

33. Murphy, interview, 22.

34. Ragland, interview, 31.

35. Christensen, interview, 21, 22.

36. Reese, interview, 10; Heneghan, interview, 33.

37. Gerwitz, interview, 19; Ragland, interview, 33; Prisock, interview, 34, 35; Murphy, interview, 23; Williams, interview, 28, 29.

38. Williams, interview, 30; Heneghan, interview, 29.

39. Murphy, interview, 25.

40. Leigh, interview, 24, 25.

41. Leigh, interview, 21.

42. Murphy, interview, 32, 33, 34.

43. McDonald, interview, 24.

44. McDonald, interview, 26.

45. Specialist Michael Babinski, interview by Kevin Hymel, Combat Studies Institute, Fort Leavenworth, KS, 31 October 2011, 13.

46. Murphy, interview, 35, 36, 37, 41, 61;

47. Prisock, interview, 49, 51, 52, 53.

48. Olson, interview, 13.

49. Leigh, interview, 21;

50. Williams, interview, 36, 37.

51. Reese, interview, 14, 15.

52. Murphy, interview, 44, 45, 46; McDonald, interview, 27; Roberts, interview, 24.

53. Williams, interview, 37, 38.

54. Stone, interview, 21.

55. Reese, interview, 17.

56. Prisock, interview, 43.

57. Davis, interview, 43.

58. Prisock, interview, 44.

59. Murphy, interview, 38.

60. Olson, interview, 15; Heneghan, interview, 47.

61. Davis, interview, 44.

62. Leigh, interview, 25, 26.

63. Rella, interview, 23.

64. Jackel, interview, 21.

65. Williams, interview, 42.

66. Williams, interview, 43, 44; Olson, interview, 20.

67. Olson, interview, 22.

68. Williams, interview, 62.

69. McDonald, interview, 29; Robert, interview, 30, 31.

70. Williams, interview, 44, 45.

71. Williams, interview, 46.

72. Olson, interview, 21, 22.

73. Williams, interview, 48, 50.

74. Christianson, interview, 30.

75. *Prisock, interview, 72.*

76. *Williams, interview, 51.*

77. *Stone, interview, 23.*

78. *Leigh, interview, 28.*

79. *Glen Goodman, "Dismounted Counter-IED: Size, Weight & Power Limits," Soldier Mod, January 2009, www.soldiermod.com/volume-2/pdfs/.../dismounted-jamming.pdf, (accessed on 13 December 2011).*

80. *Christianson, interview, 30, 31.*

81. *Prisock, interview, 71; McDonald, interview, 31, 32.*

82. *Gerwitz, interview, 33; Stone, interview, 25.*

83. *McDonald, interview, 32, 33.*

84. *Prisock, interview, 63, 64, 76.*

85. *Murphy, interview, 59; Babinski, interview, 20.*

86. *McDonald, interview, 34.*

87. *Lieutenant Taylor Murphy, e-mail to Kevin Hymel, Combat Studies Institute, Fort Leavenworth, KS, 31 January 2012.*

88. *Murphy, interview, 56.*

89. *Babinski, interview, 20, 21.*

90. *Roberts, interview, 36.*

91. *Babinski, interview, 22.*

92. *Prisock, interview, 65.*

93. *Prisock, interview, 72.*

94. *Christensen, interview, 38.*

95. *Murphy, interview, 57, 58; Williams, interview, 52.*

96. *Prisock, interview, 74; Olson, interview, 26; Ragland, interview, 45; Williams, interview, 51.*

97. *McDonald, interview, 38, 39.*

98. *Murphy, interview, 59, 60.*

99. *McDonald, interview, 38.*

100. *Babinski, interview, 27, 33.*

101. *Leigh, interview, 38, 40.*

102. *Murphy, interview, 63; Babinski, interview, 25, 30.*

103. *Rella, interview, 45.*

104. *Stone, interview, 27.*

105. Ragland, interview, 56.

106. Prisock, interview, 77; Stone, interview, 29.

107. Gerwitz, interview, 37.

108. Ragland, interview, 59.

109. Babinski, interview, 29.

110. Davis, interview, 51, 52.

111. Prisock, interview, 80.

112. Roberts, interview, 43.

113. Murphy, interview, 67.

114. Williams, interview, 57.

115. Jackel, interview, 33.

116. McDonald, interview, 46.

117. Williams, interview, 59.

118. Davis, interview, 56.

119. Captain James Prisock, e-mail to Kevin M. Hymel, Combat Studies Institute, Fort Leavenworth, KS, 5 January 2012.

120. Ragland, interview, 27; Murphy, interview, 30; Leigh, interview, 42; Gerwitz, interview, 44.

121. Stone, interview, 3.

122. Williams, interview, 25.

123. Roberts, interview, 49.

124. Olson, interview, 27.

125. Stone, interview, 16.

126. Christensen, interview, 27.

127. Leigh, interview, 46.

128. Gerwitz, interview, 18.

129. Roberts, interview, 29.

130. Jackel, interview, 40.

131. Williams, interview, 72.

132. Stone, interview, 20.

133. Heneghan, interview, 48.

134. Stone, interview, 39.

135. Davis, interview, 14.

136. Davis, interview, 59; Prisock, e-mail.

Gaining the Initiative in Musahi
Using CERP to Disrupt the Taliban
in Kabul Province
by
Anthony E. Carlson, Ph. D.

In October 2010, Taliban insurgents controlled the Musahi valley in east-central Afghanistan. Nestled between Logar Province to the south and the Afghan capital of Kabul to the north, the valley was a strategic Taliban corridor. Located 25 kilometers southeast of Kabul, the Musahi District had a population of 44,000 residents scattered throughout 22 villages.[1] Waging a ruthless campaign of intimidation and violence, the Taliban terrorized the Musahi population, established a string of weapons caches, assassinated and kidnapped members of the Afghan National Police (ANP), bribed local government officials, and detonated roadside improvised explosive devices (IEDs) throughout the valley. The Musahi ANP proved incapable of protecting the population or ending the Taliban's reign of terror. Outmanned, undersupplied, inexperienced, and crippled by desertions, the ANP seldom ventured away from their security checkpoints. As a result, the Taliban controlled the valley with little resistance. Eleven years after the US-led invasion of Afghanistan, the deteriorating security situation on the doorstep of the national capital defied simple solutions.[2]

In late 2010, the daunting task of professionalizing the valley's ANP fell to the Musahi Police Mentor Team (PMT). Under the direction of First Lieutenant Dennis Frey, Jr., the PMT, comprised of 13 Soldiers from the Nebraska Army National Guard's Alpha Troop, 1st Squadron, 134th Cavalry Regiment (A/1-134 CAV), arrived at Camp Dubbs in Kabul in November and assessed Musahi's grave security situation. Frey decided to launch a large-scale humanitarian aid (HA) mission funded by the Commander's Emergency Response Program (CERP). A Department of Defense (DOD) program, CERP distributed humanitarian and reconstruction money to US military commanders with minimal bureaucratic interference. Although CERP generally provided support to humanitarian and reconstruction initiatives, Frey expanded the program's role in Musahi. The objective of his CERP-funded HA mission was twofold. First, Frey hoped that a surge of humanitarian and medical assistance might win the hearts and minds of Musahi residents and turn them against the Taliban. Second, given the PMT's limited manpower, the HA deliveries required the participation of ANP personnel. Frey thus envisioned the HA deliveries as on-the-job training for untrained and beleaguered local policemen. In conducting the deliveries, the Musahi PMT mentored the ANP on how to establish inner and outer security cordons, detain insurgents, and conduct mounted and dismounted patrols. The combined HA and police mentoring missions yielded immediate dividends. Emboldened by a resurgent and engaged police force, Musahi residents rose up against Taliban oppression. Villagers provided intelligence about the location of weapons caches, identified smuggling routes, confronted armed bands of Taliban insurgents, and invited Alpha Troop Soldiers into their homes. For the first time in the war, the Taliban were on the defensive in the Musahi valley.[3]

As Alpha Troop's nine-month deployment concluded in the summer of 2011, First Lieutenant Frey's creative and improvised use of CERP funds transformed the Musahi ANP into a functional police force, galvanized the valley's population against the insurgency, and tilted the balance of power in favor of coalition forces. The PMT's mentoring and security achievements testified to Frey's ambitious leadership and initiative, helping disrupt a Taliban stronghold without the firing of a single bullet. CERP proved a valuable weapon in confronting an elusive, ruthless, and determined adversary.

The Genesis and Evolution of CERP

CERP originated due to an unlikely discovery during Operation IRAQI FREEDOM. Shortly after the overthrow of Saddam Hussein's regime in the spring of 2003, 3d Infantry Division (Mechanized) Soldiers discovered sealed stacks of $100 bills in the palaces of former Ba'athist party officials. Over the next few weeks, US Soldiers discovered additional cash stashes in dog kennels and other locations that increased the stockpiles' value to more than $700 million (USD). Accountants and auditors later concluded that the money had been embezzled from the United Nations' (UN) Oil for Food program. Given the unclear legal status of the seized cash, the US Central Command (CENTCOM) reserved the money as the property of Iraqi citizens.[4]

US Commanders identified the cash hoards as a key enabler to build a new Iraq. Predictably, the 2003 invasion of Iraq disrupted basic utility and sanitation services, prompted food and water shortages, wrecked the country's already dilapidated infrastructure, and led to a deepening humanitarian crisis. After toppling the Hussein regime, US Army commanders had no funds at their disposal to initiate urgent humanitarian, reconstruction, or infrastructure projects. Recognizing these shortcomings, Lieutenant General Ricardo Sanchez, the Combined Joint Task Force-7

(CJTF-7) commander, asked Ambassador Paul Bremer to release the sequestered funds to the commander of Coalition Forces. On June 16, 2003, Bremer complied, empowering the commander to "take all actions necessary to operate a Commanders' Emergency Response Program." Within sixteen months, Coalitions forces had spent $578 million in CERP funds to underwrite agriculture, cleanup, education, electric, health care, irrigation, rule of law, sanitation, telecommunication, transportation, and water projects throughout Iraq.[5]

US Commanders in Iraq celebrated CERP's responsiveness, flexibility, and adaptability to diverse local conditions. The program enabled tactical units to complete urgent, targeted, and low-level projects with minimal bureaucratic delays. Indeed, a handful of early reports suggested a link between secure Iraqi communities and high levels of CERP funding.[6] CERP's popularity and track record of promoting local stability led Congress, in late 2003, to extend the program to Afghanistan and begin making annual appropriations. As of 30 September 2011, Congress had appropriated a total of $3.04 billion for CERP projects in Iraq and Afghanistan.[7]

CERP emerged as a critical weapon in the counterinsurgency (COIN) campaign in Afghanistan. Revised in February 2011, *Money as a Weapon System – Afghanistan*, a United States Forces-Afghanistan (USFOR-A) publication, defined the objectives, purpose, intent, and standard operating procedure (SOP) of CERP. The CERP SOP stipulated that "the purpose of the CERP is to enable US commanders to respond to urgent **humanitarian relief** and **reconstruction** requirements within their Area of Responsibility (AOR) by carrying out programs that will immediately assist the indigenous population."[8] The SOP defined "urgent" as "any chronic or acute inadequacy of an essential good or service that, in the judgment of the **local commander**, calls for action."[9] Low-level projects that provided "urgent humanitarian relief" or afforded "significant employment opportunities" deserved priority. The SOP directed commanders to confirm that funding from the Government of the Islamic Republic of Afghanistan (GIRoA), nongovernmental organizations (NGOs), donor nation, or other humanitarian aid sources was unavailable before initiating a funding request.[10]

In Afghanistan, CERP's quick-impact philosophy supported coalition force's effort to deepen and expand GIRoA's influence. Encouraging US commanders to initiate projects that could be rapidly completed, enjoyed high visibility, cost less than $500,000, addressed chronic unemployment, and were sustainable by local or provincial governments,

CERP constituted a non-lethal weapon system dedicated to winning the hearts and minds of Afghan citizens. Seeking to increase the tempo of Afghan reconstruction, the CERP SOP prohibited funding in many circumstances: providing funds, goods, or services to US military personnel; weapons buy-back programs; reward programs; removal of IEDs or other unexploded ordinance; paying bonuses, salaries, or pensions of Afghan civil or military personnel; equipping or training ANP or Afghan National Army (ANA) units; conducting psychological or information operations; directly supporting Afghan individuals or private businesses (notwithstanding condolence payments, battle damage, or former detainee reparations). Urgent humanitarian and reconstruction needs remained CERP's paramount objective.[11]

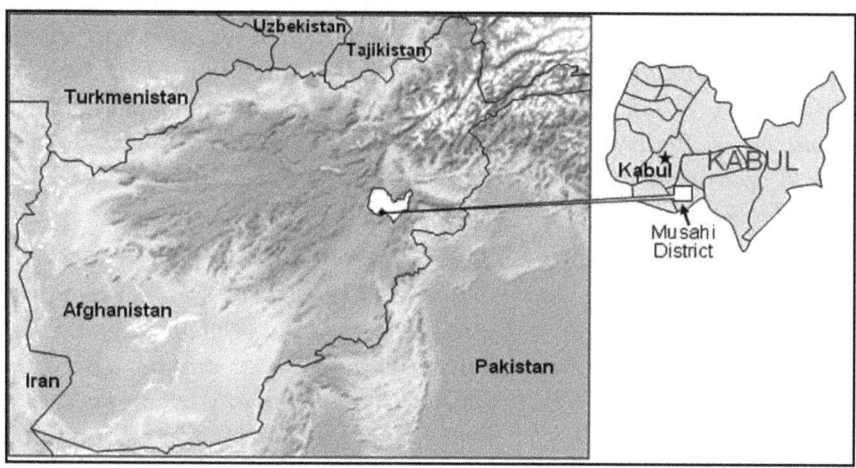

Figure 1. Kabul Province and the Musahi District.

The Musahi Valley in 2010

Given CERP's goals, Alpha Troop Soldiers identified the Musahi valley as an ideal funding candidate. Early in their deployment, the Soldiers diagnosed multiple economic and social problems. By the end of 2010, the valley's stagnant rural economy, chronic poverty, widespread illiteracy, lack of living necessities (such as winter clothing and food staples), dilapidated infrastructure, and absence of economic and educational opportunities fueled an acute humanitarian crisis. Recent environmental disasters magnified the impoverished populace's suffering. During the previous spring, rapid snowmelt overwhelmed the tributaries of the Logar River, the major watercourse dissecting the Musahi district, submerging wheat and barley fields. Since most residents cultivated small irrigated plots, the flooding constituted a significant economic hardship.[12]

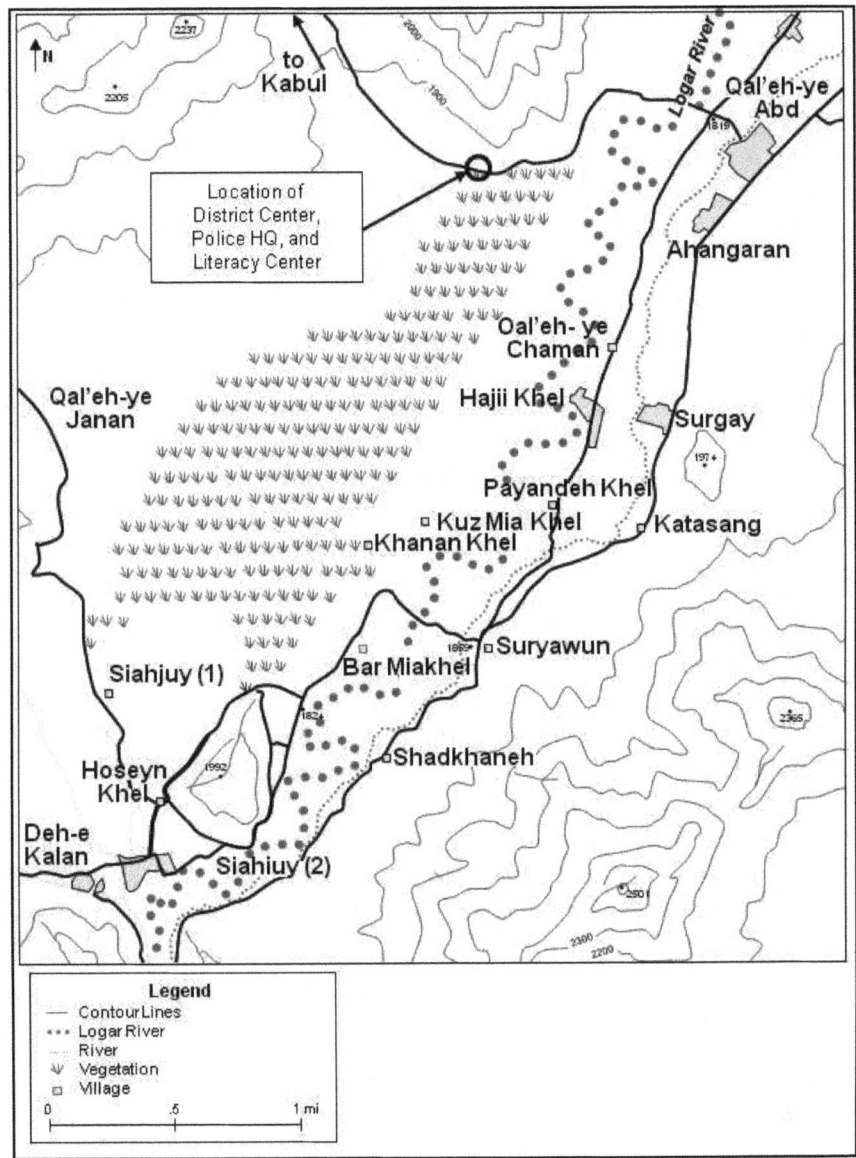

Figure 2. The Musahi valley.

The Musahi district government proved unresponsive to the economic and security crises. Villagers told Staff Sergeant Christopher Marcello, the Musahi PMT's noncommissioned officer in charge (NCOIC), that local police or security forces had not conducted mounted or dismounted patrols south of the Logar River in more than two decades. Logistical and professional shortcomings hampered the ANP's effectiveness. Distant from government supply warehouses, which catered to urban police elements, the Musahi ANP was undersupplied, underequipped, and untrained. The Taliban exploited these structural weaknesses by targeting local policemen for kidnappings, assassinations, and ambushes. An ANP Lieutenant named Sanayee, a company commander in the Police Battalion responsible for the Musahi region, stated in early 2011 that "I've been attacked six times by explosives and five times through ambushes. [Musahi] is the worst place I have worked."[13] Alleged drug use and a lack of professionalism undermined the ANP's morale and confidence. Unwilling to stray from checkpoints, the Musahi ANP seldom interacted with local residents. The valley's notoriety as a hotbed of Taliban activity spread, making it difficult for the ANP to recruit new officers, curb desertions, and engage the population. Although the Musahi ANP was on paper staffed at 120 police officers, it seldom employed more than 40-50 full-time policemen at any given time. Even more alarming were intelligence reports suggesting that 90 percent of the local police force sympathized with or were on the Taliban payroll.[14]

Poverty and dysfunctional governance intensified the Taliban insurgency. Moving unfettered throughout Musahi, the Taliban established weapons caches, planted roadside bombs, transformed the valley into a smuggling "gateway" and "alleyway" from Logar Province into Kabul, and unleashed a hostile propaganda campaign. The negligible police presence allowed the Taliban to show up at villagers' homes and demand safe haven after sundown. The Taliban also intimidated government officials and cultivated a network of local informants. Each passing day of inaction worsened the grim security situation, jeopardizing stability in the national capital.[15]

CERP in Musahi: A Lesson in Creative and Independent Leadership

On 27 July 2010, General David H. Petraeus, the commander of the International Security Assistance Force (ISAF) and USFOR-A, issued the COMISAF's Counterinsurgency Guidance. In the document, Petraeus argued that "the Taliban are not the only enemy of the [Afghan] people. The people are also threatened by inadequate governance, corruption, and abuse of power—the Taliban's best recruiters ... Work with our Afghan partners to help ... protect the people from malign actors as well as from terrorists."[16] Musahi was a case study in the social and political ills that Petraeus described. The Taliban capitalized on Musahi's ineffective governance, corruption, and economic calamities at the expense of the local population.

In late 2010, the 1-134 CAV, christened Task Force Fury, took responsibility for fortifying security in Kabul Province. Arriving in Afghanistan on 13 November, Task Force Fury was a Cavalry Reconnaissance and Surveillance (R&S) Squadron that had approximately 370 Soldiers and fell under USFOR-A's Regional Command Capital (RC-Capital). The R&S squadron consisted of A, B, and C Troops and a Headquarters and Headquarters Troop (HHT). In preparing to conduct its primary mission of mentoring the ANP and ANA, the task force divided Kabul Province into four separate "police zones." Each 1-134 CAV troop was assigned to an individual police zone. Zone 1, encompassing three ANP precincts in Kabul City and the volatile Musahi district, belonged to Alpha Troop.[17]

The Musahi PMT welcomed their daunting assignment. Composed of 13 Alpha Troop Soldiers, a medic, and two interpreters, the PMT was a hybrid, ad hoc entity. First Lieutenant Dennis Frey, Jr., was the PMT's officer in charge (OIC). As a Nebraska State Patrolman at the time of Alpha Troop's deployment, Frey was the perfect candidate to lead the PMT, bringing to the team valuable civilian experience in search procedures, report protocols, patrol techniques, arrest and detainment skills, and other police-related activities. Subordinates described Frey, a veteran of Operation IRAQI FREEDOM, as an assertive, diligent, purposeful, and adaptive leader who excelled at mediating conflicts and communicating with diverse groups. Staff Sergeant Marcello, a veteran of the Kosovo intervention and Operation IRAQI FREEDOM, was the PMT's NCOIC. Staff Sergeant Michael Belleci served as the senior scout and Sergeant Randall Barnason was the "squad leader," responsible for the remaining enlisted Soldiers. The PMT traveled on three Mine Resistant Ambush Protected (MRAP) All-Terrain Vehicles (M-ATVs), armed either with M240B or M2 .50 caliber machine guns. During initial patrols in the Musahi valley, Frey's PMT discovered no police presence outside of isolated checkpoints. Furthermore, he immediately recognized that proper police instruction was useless as long as ANP personnel sequestered themselves behind security checkpoints and in the district police headquarters (HQ) compound. The ANP needed to earn the respect and trust of the local population before they could become an efficient police organization.[18]

Frey seized the initiative by immersing himself in Musahi tribal politics. Cultural awareness was a prerequisite for US company grade officers to spearhead successful police mentoring, HA, and COIN missions. Understanding the importance of the local culture and Afghan tribal politics, Frey attended his first Musahi shura in December 2010. In Afghan tribal culture, shuras were periodic council meetings that arbitrated local conflicts and oversaw issues related to agriculture, humanitarian needs, infrastructure, justice, law and order, reconstruction, and security.[9] In Frey's apt description, shuras resembled "open town hall forums" where village elders made routine governance decisions.[20] Winning the hearts and minds of Musahi residents and fortifying police protection began at the village level.

Frey's unannounced attendance at a December shura with the local ANP chief made tribal elders uncomfortable and apprehensive. Isolated, impoverished, and suspicious of outsiders, Musahi leaders had minimal contact with GIRoA, NGOs, US Soldiers, the ANP, or other international aid organizations. Looking to defuse the tense encounter, Frey removed his body armor and remained silent. As the shura continued, Frey observed, through his interpreter, that a "common theme" of discussion was a "lack of jobs, a lack of education, a lack of food, [and] a lack of warm clothing."[21] Besieged by a cruel insurgency and lacking basic living supplies, Musahi women and children required basic necessities just to survive the harsh winter months. Tribal elders also bemoaned the fact that overcrowded schools, few educational supplies, and ramshackle school buildings deprived their children of the possibility of a prosperous future. For Frey, CERP provided an opportunity to address these humanitarian and social shortcomings. Rather than viewing HA as an entitlement for destitute Afghan villagers, Frey touted the program as a motivational tool capable of choking off Taliban influence at the grassroots. Small wonder Frey believed that Musahi's short-term stability depended as much on a surge of humanitarian assistance as an efficient police force.[22]

After the shura, Frey met with his commander, Captain Zachary Labrayere, about Musahi's humanitarian crisis. Surprised by his subordinate's initiative, Labrayere encouraged Frey to do everything possible to alleviate the valley's suffering, broaden the coalition's presence, and improve the ANP's tactical awareness and proficiency. Frey promoted the valley as an ideal CERP candidate. Coordinating with Captain Jeremy Syznskie, the 1-134 CAV's civil-military officer (S9), Frey learned the process of requesting and procuring CERP funding. The first step in the process was for Musahi government officials to fill out documentation requesting humanitarian assistance stamped with the local government's seal. At a subsequent shura, Frey presented the paperwork to village elders. A week later, the elders submitted a stamped request for basic food staples (rice, beans, sugar, flour, cooking oil) and winter clothing (coats, blankets, gloves, and so forth). The positive response pleased Frey. If awarded money to buy HA supplies, he intended to use the humanitarian mission as an opportunity to cultivate goodwill with valley residents and mentor the ANP in standard police procedures.[23]

According to Captain Szynskie, the Musahi humanitarian mission fit the CERP funding criteria. Once Frey notified Syznskie of his intention to request CERP funding, the proposal went through the standard nominating process. The first step involved completing a project nominating form. On this form, Frey listed the grid location, village names, type of project, and sponsoring local elder. Frey then submitted the paperwork to the squadron S9 section. At this point, Szynskie took the nominating form before the squadron Project Review Board (PRB). Convening every two to three weeks, the PRB evaluated CERP nominations from all four 1-134 CAV police zones. Composed of squadron commander Lieutenant Colonel Thomas Rynders, Syzenskie, the S9 section, the squadron executive officer (XO), and PMT leaders, the PRB made final CERP decisions. Although Rynders exercised exclusive authority over project selections, the PRB generally endorsed Syznskie's recommendations, which adhered to the CERP SOP guidelines: addressing urgent humanitarian crises and providing employment opportunities to Afghan citizens. [24]

After the selection of a CERP project, the 1-134 CAV's four program managers (each responsible for one of the four police zones) initiated the requisite documentation and solicited bids. This process required completing a project letter of justification (LOJ) and filling out a Combined Information Data Network Exchange (CIDNE) report. Among other functions, CIDNE was a DOD database that tracked CERP projects and stored uploaded documents. The signing of both documents by the commander, in Szynskie's words, was "kind of like receiving the order to go ahead and move forward" with the project.[5] At that point, the project manager completed a "statement of understanding," signed by the squadron commander and the appropriate Afghan ministry, and a "statement of work," which explained what a contractor needed to do as part of the project. Once the forms were collected and compiled, the project went out for bid. The S9 office maintained a specific e-mail account that disseminated projects to local contractors. E-mail notifications generally identified the project location, requirements listed in the statement of work, and the bidding deadline. Prior to the bid closing date, contractors delivered their bids, in sealed envelopes, to security guards at the front gate of Camp Phoenix in Kabul. The guards then placed the sealed bids in a secure mailbox. After the deadline passed, the squadron S9 collected, evaluated, compared, and awarded the "best value" bid. After notifying *the winning contractor, the CERP project commenced, supervised by the appropriate project manager.*[6]

As Frey anticipated, the Musahi HA CERP request received early approval. Because many HA supplies were donated through the US-based Operation Outreach Afghanistan (OOA), CERP did not fund the entire HA package. Nevertheless, the PMT leader began to plan for the HA deliveries using a needs-based distribution strategy. Consulting with the Musahi police chief, Frey identified the five poorest villages to receive the deliveries. He always intended for the HA deliveries to serve a dual purpose. First, they were the initial step in winning the trust of Musahi residents and disrupting the Taliban's stranglehold. In the long run, Frey hoped that the HA distributions might encourage residents to provide actionable intelligence on Taliban informants living amidst the population, weapons stockpiles, roadside IEDs, and potential ambushes.

Second, the HA deliveries also constituted a police training exercise. CERP SOP prohibited funds from equipping, training, or underwriting the costs associated with ANP operations but the HA deliveries did require security. Using the ANP to establish security perimeters, search incoming vehicles, conduct foot patrols, and distribute goods as part of the HA deliveries served the broader purpose of the PMT mission. After selecting the delivery locations, Frey emphasized to the police chief that the PMT intended to take a "backseat" during the deliveries. "We really wanted the Afghan police chief to take ownership of the mission," Frey explained, "to set this thing up and to really run with it."[27]

The PMT's innovative approach broadened CERP's functional utility beyond traditional reconstruction and humanitarian emphases. Indeed, CERP's streamlined and decentralized framework liberated company grade officers to make decisions that allowed them to gain the initiative during low-level tactical operations. In the hands of creative and innovative officers, money in the form of CERP assistance became a powerful enabler for localized COIN and police mentoring efforts.

Operation UNITED FRONT I

The HA deliveries served as on-the-job training for the ANP. Upon selecting the time and location of the HA drops, Frey coordinated security and manpower requirements with the police chief. According to the PMT leader, the HA drops were "where we really made our money with mentoring the police."[28] On the mornings of the scheduled drops, the PMT showed up at the district police headquarters, rounded up available ANP officers, formed a vehicle convoy, and traveled to the predetermined *drop destinations. After arriving at the site, Staff Sergeant Marcello and Alpha Troop Soldiers mentored the ANP in setting up outer and inner security cordons, placing concertina wire, conducting foot patrols, searching vehicles, and patting down villagers. Frey also insisted that the ANP take the lead in distributing the HA supplies. It was critical that the local population perceive the drops as evidence of a newly engaged and generous local government committed to their welfare. Attempting to bolster security, Staff Sergeant Belleci operated a Raven unmanned aerial vehicle (UAV) to provide overhead surveillance. The Raven UAV had a wingspan of nearly five feet and transmitted color video images over a range of seven miles.[29]*

Figure 3. An ANP Officer Distributes HA Supplies in the Mushai valley.
Photo Courtesy of First Lieutenant Sean Polson

Ensuring that the HA goods made it into the hands of impoverished villagers was crucial for mission success. Sometime during 2010, Soldiers from the Massachusetts Army National Guard 101st Field Artillery Regiment had arranged an HA delivery for the Musahi district. Rather than distributing the supplies throughout the valley, corrupt ANP personnel allegedly stole the items for their own families. The abortive delivery eroded the ANP's credibility and trustworthiness and was a repeated topic of discussion in Musahi shuras. Committed to avoiding a replay of the previous year's scandalous and counterproductive HA delivery, the PMT provided maximum security, exercised strict oversight, and demanded accountability from ANP officers. The PMT intended to rebuild trust between villagers and the ANP. Since any security incidences or rumors of police graft would further alienate the population from the local government, corruption was not tolerated.³⁰

The HA deliveries commenced on 27 December 2010 at Qal'eh-ye Abd. Codenamed Operation UNITED FRONT I, the deliveries distributed at least 25 tons of humanitarian goods to the Musahi valley's five poorest villages (Qal'eh-ye-Abd, Qeshlaqe Ul'ya, Qal'eh-ye Janan, Shadkbaneh, and Katasang).³¹ Families received a blanket, a tarp, jackets, gloves, socks, shoes, underwear, a portable iron stove, charcoal, a 4-liter bottle of cooking oil, sugar, salt, and 5-pound sacks of beans, flour, and rice. The PMT also passed out personal hygiene items: shaving cream, soap, tooth brushes, and toothpaste. Children were given candy and basic school supplies. Afghans praised the deliveries. Sardar Mahammad, a Musahi unskilled laborer whose family participated in a 6 February distribution, observed that "it would take me five days of work to earn enough money to buy what we were given today."³²

Figure 4. A Musahi Child Clutches a Blanket Received during an HA Delivery.
Photo Courtesy of First Lieutenant Sean Polson

Villagers' attitude towards coalition forces improved following the HA deliveries. In the past, valley residents either retreated into their homes if they observed approaching US Soldiers or hurled rocks and insults. Terrified of Taliban retribution, villagers avoided any contact with

US soldiers. Nevertheless, during the HA deliveries, villagers temporarily overcame their fear of Taliban reprisals, deciding that the reward of free supplies outweighed the risk of insurgent violence. Ultimately, it was difficult to assess whether Musahi villagers' newfound conciliatory disposition towards coalition forces reflected narrow opportunism or an unequivocal rejection of Taliban ideology. In the short-term, however, the results of the HA deliveries met Frey's expectations. Rather than pelting passing M-ATVs with stones or hurling invective at coalition and ANP personnel, Musahi children now rushed to greet them with smiles and open arms.[33]

The HA deliveries were only part of a broader effort to improve short- and long-term social conditions in the valley. In conjunction with the HA drops, the PMT orchestrated the CERP-funded construction and improvement of two schools. By paying local contractors to renovate existing schools and build new structures, the PMT created temporary construction jobs and permanent opportunities for unemployed Musahi educators. Built in the spring of 2011, the Shad-e-Kana School contained eight classrooms, a new drinking water well, and two five-stall open pit latrines. Located near the Musahi police HQ, the completed school educated 1,000 Afghans at a total construction cost of $200,000. CERP also funded the renovation of the Khuwajah Dalil village school. The project replaced a failing roof with corrugated sheet metal, constructed two new latrines, and erected a second eight-classroom building. Once completed, the renovations totaled $250,000.[34]

The PMT also launched two medical air drops during the winter. Funded by CERP, the drops occurred about five miles south of the Musahi Police HQ. The PMT purchased the supplies, which totaled $19,600, from a Kabul pharmacy based on a list submitted by the Afghan Ministry of Health to the squadron's S9. Consisting mostly of non-prescription items, the drops delivered IV bags, upper respiratory medication, powdered milk, infant medication, cough syrup, Tylenol, antibiotics, and other medical supplies. The medical drops corrected a vital medical supply shortage and met an urgent humanitarian need. According to First Lieutenant Dain Miller, the Zone 1 CERP project manager, the medical supply distributions, along with Operation UNITED FRONT I, had a "positive impact" with the local population and gave them a reason to rise up against the Taliban's heavy-handed tactics.[35]

Prevailing US COIN doctrine cast robust indigenous insurgencies as a product of quantifiable economic and social imbalances. The infusion of HA and medical supplies into Musahi sought to correct these imbalances *and, as a positive consequence, disrupt the Taliban's hold over valley communities. An isolated incident suggested that the Musahi PMT's humanitarian emphasis led to measurable security improvements. During one of the final HA deliveries, a band of Taliban insurgents, armed with rocket propelled grenades (RPGs) and RPK machine guns, planned to assault US Soldiers and ANP personnel. Learning about the imminent attack, a group of Musahi villagers banded together and collectively confronted the armed insurgents. Villagers demanded that the insurgents throw down their weapons, leave the area, and allow the distribution to proceed. Jolted by the angry mob's assertiveness, the insurgents departed without incident. The PMT and ANP had started to turn the tide against the Taliban.*[36]

Securing the Musahi Valley

The results of the HA deliveries now exceeded Frey's expectations. As the distributions continued, crowds grew in size and enthusiasm. Attendance at shuras also increased. Grateful for the assistance, Musahi residents invited Alpha Troop Soldiers into their homes and welcomed their presence as a bulwark against Taliban persecution. Since hospitality was an indispensible part of Afghan culture, Frey and his Soldiers never refused an opportunity to build solidarity with villagers. By the middle of February, routine PMT patrols often ended with Alpha Troop Soldiers sipping tea and eating bread inside of villagers' homes. Once despised as unwelcome intruders and occupiers, Alpha Troop relished the population's new friendly and accommodating disposition.[37]

Operation UNITED FRONT I was the catalyst for beginning to clear the Taliban from Musahi. Given the PMT's limited manpower and resources, Frey realized that it was a pipedream to completely eliminate the Taliban's influence and freedom of movement over such a wide geographic area. The PMT only intended to disrupt the insurgency's stranglehold and limit insurgent mobility. By March 2011, Frey worked to translate the goodwill and credibility generated by the humanitarian deliveries into tangible security gains. During a March luncheon attended by key tribal elders and hosted by the police chief, Frey implored attendees to strike a fatal blow against the insurgency by proving information about the location of Taliban IED factories, weapons caches, and informants. The elders met Frey's challenge. On 14 March, an elder identified the location of a weapons stockpile that contained RPGs, mortars, and various other munitions. After securing and cordoning off the cache, the 1-134 CAV's route clearance team seized the munitions, transported them to a remote location, and detonated them.[38]

Intelligence also flowed into the 1-134 CAV's public affairs element about Taliban sympathizers. According to First Lieutenant Sean Polson, the squadron CERP purchasing officer, the tightening bonds between the Musahi population and coalition forces led to the identification of a local religious leader that regularly assisted the Taliban. The PMT questioned the Malik about his role within the insurgency and scanned his fingerprints, photograph, and retinal data into the Biometric Automated Toolset (BAT) System, a DOD database that stores the biometric data of suspected insurgents. Although the Malik was not arrested since his name did not appear in the BAT database, Polson expounded on the episode's significance. "Just being able to get that kind of information out of the community," he insisted, "was a positive step in the right direction."[39] *Unfortunately, the Taliban, weary about losing their stranglehold over a key smuggling corridor into the national capital, planned a savage reprisal. The ANP's budding resolve and professionalism would soon be tested.*[40]

The Taliban Strike Back

On the morning of 14 April, a Taliban insurgent slammed a dump truck loaded with 600 to 1,000 pounds of homemade explosives (HME) into the Musahi District Government Center and adjacent ANP HQ. The explosives detonated and leveled the compound. Flying shrapnel sliced through the building and rendered it uninhabitable. Polson compared the damaged compound to a block of "Swiss cheese" or the Alfred P. Murrah Federal Building in the aftermath of the 1995 Oklahoma City bombing. Fortunately, the brazen suicide attack claimed but a single fatality: the suicide bomber. A safety barrier wall absorbed much of the blast and shielded the police HQ, saving the lives of countless sleeping Afghan policemen.[41]

Ironically, at the time of the attack, Alpha Troop Soldiers were taking a scheduled physical fitness exam in Kabul. After learning about the explosion, Soldiers quickly donned their gear, drove to the site of the blast, established a security perimeter, and commenced the initial recovery. The timing of the suicide attack surprised no one. Over the previous weeks, the Taliban had issued a steady stream of verbal and written threats directed against the police chief and ANP for cooperating with coalition forces. "The Taliban's attack on the Musahi District Government Center," Miller argued, was a "direct result of their perceived loss of power [within] the communities throughout Musahi."[42] *The fact that the HME load, concealed in the dump truck by a pile of firewood, navigated through security and observation checkpoints undetected revealed the limited nature of the*

Figure 5. Musahi Taliban Weapons Cache.
Photo Courtesy of First Lieutenant Sean Polson

Figure 6. The Wreckage of the Musahi District Government Center.

Photo Courtesy of First Lieutenant Sean Polson

ANP's improved professionalism and situational awareness. The Taliban retained the ability to launch spectacular attacks intended to hamper the local government's ability to function.[43]

The attack marked a pivotal moment. Having felt the force of the explosion and witnessed billowing smoke clouds, Musahi residents assumed that the blast cut the entire ANP force to pieces. Taliban propaganda portrayed the blast as a decisive victory. Indeed, the valley's lack of telecommunication networks made the population vulnerable to such exaggerated claims. Cut off from the flow of information, most Musahi villagers received news from neighbors, friends, or relatives. Frightened residents now concluded that the price of cooperating with coalition forces or the ANP was death. To make matters worse, the explosion led a sizable number of ANP personnel to desert. The Musahi valley teetered on the brink of a Taliban resurgence.

Unless the ANP established an immediate presence throughout the valley, the PMT worried that the suicide attack might reverse the limited security gains. Seizing the initiative, Frey and Marcello implored the police chief to dispatch policemen throughout the valley. The chief responded with resolute determination. Before the end of the day, the ANP, backed *by PMT Soldiers, conducted patrols, manned security checkpoints, and established a police presence throughout the valley. The sight of the ANP patrolling astonished Musahi residents, who thought the entire police force was slaughtered or, at the very best, cowering behind observation posts. The suicide attack on the district government center proved counterproductive because the ANP demonstrated its growing resolve and commitment to protecting the population in the face of violence. The police chief's quick response and forceful leadership nullified the effects of the blast.*[44]

Operation UNITED FRONT II

The suicide attack triggered Operation UNITED FRONT II. Following the three-month conclusion of Operation UNITED FRONT I, Frey and Captain Labrayere discussed strategies to expand the coalition force's reach and further marginalize the Taliban. They conceived of a plan to go door-to-door through every Musahi village, collecting demographic, religious, and economic information from the head of each household. Since US Soldiers had never conducted a census of Afghans in the isolated valley or ventured south of the Logar River, they knew precious little about the valley's population, ethnicity, or religious preferences. Gathering such information was critical to meeting the future humanitarian needs and determining appropriate numbers of school classrooms or medical clinics. The door-to-door contacts also allowed Musahi villagers to interact with coalition and ANP personnel. When Frey proposed the plan in March to the police chief, he was apprehensive and hesitant. As Frey recalled, the chief did not want to have "coalition soldiers in the middle of all these villages on foot, doing foot patrols and going door to door, and really getting in the weeds with all of the village members."[45] *He feared that the PMT, by venturing too far into isolated and inward looking villages, might present the faulty impression that the local government was a puppet of the US military. Since Frey intended for the ANP to spearhead the door-to-door mission, the police chief's reluctance led the PMT to shelve the plan.*

The police chief reversed course after the leveling of the district government center. Intelligence reports indicated that the suicide attack constituted an unsuccessful assassination attempt on the chief. Fearful of the Taliban's tenacity and resilience, he acquiesced and provided Frey with the manpower and resources to carry out Operation UNITED FRONT II. In late April, the ANP and PMT divided into three teams and executed the three-week operation. Each team conducted mounted and dismounted foot patrols in every Musahi village during the census. Assisted by ANP personnel and interpreters, the PMT Soldiers knocked on doors, spoke to the heads of households, and then asked standard demographic questions: occupation, ethnic affiliation, religious background, number of children, identity of local religious leaders, and place of worship. In general, the door-to-door visitations proceeded without any violence. Villagers answered the questions and sometimes even welcomed Soldiers into their homes for tea. On a few isolated occasions, residents threatened Soldiers or pointedly offered to feed them "poisoned" food. Despite these isolated threats, Operation UNITED FRONT II succeeded in completing the first comprehensive census ever taken in the Musahi district.[46]

The ANP's broadened presence yielded other security triumphs. During Operation UNITED FRONT II, which lasted until mid-May, locals provided ANP and Alpha Troop Soldiers intelligence about or discovered the location of eight previously unknown Taliban weapons caches. In sum, 640 pounds of HME, 13 RPGs, 12 anti-personnel mines, and other ordnance were taken into US custody. In the aftermath of the suicide blast, Musahi residents remained resolute.[47]

Prior to Alpha Troop's departure in July, Frey requested a final CERP project. During shuras, elders complained that the valley's low literacy rate hampered residents' employment opportunities in Kabul, made the population vulnerable to Taliban propaganda, and inhibited the ANP from effective written communication with one another. Indeed, in 2002, the Office of the United Nations High Commissioner for Refugees (UNHCR) estimated that barely one in five Musahi residents were literate.[48] *Written records were a precondition for establishing and maintaining a functional system of law and order. Seeking to boost the indigenous literacy rate, Frey requested the construction of a CERP-funded adult literacy center next to the police HQ to teach Dari and Pashto. Captain Szynskie initially hesitated to authorize the undertaking since "the location was near Police Headquarters and I was concerned that only the police would be able to attend classes. CERP is to be used exclusively for the civilian populace, not the Army or Police units."*[49] *After Frey secured assurances from district elders that the literacy center was to serve the entire district, and not just the ANP, Szynskie approved the project on 19 June. The Musahi government donated land near the leveled district government compound for the literacy center. As Alpha Troop Soldiers left Afghanistan, contractors commenced the initial dirt and leveling work at the construction site.*[50]

Aftermath

The US Army's doctrine of Full Spectrum Operations guided the Soldiers of Alpha Troop. As explained in Field Manual 3-0, Operations, full spectrum operations were the combination of "offensive, defensive, and stability ... operations [conducted] simultaneously as part of an interdependent joint force to seize, retain, and exploit the initiative, accepting prudent risk to create opportunities to achieve decisive results.[51] *In these operations, individual Soldiers bore responsibility for gaining the initiative. "Seizing, retaining, and exploiting the initiative," the manual emphasized, "depend[ed] on individual initiative—the willingness to act in the absence of orders, when existing orders no longer fit the situation, or when unforeseen opportunities ... arise."*[52] *In Afghanistan, opportunistic officers had many lethal and non-lethal opportunities to seize and hold the initiative. As Lieutenant Frey discovered, one of the most promising, and often overlooked, opportunities involved humanitarian assistance missions.*

In the Musahi valley, CERP funds empowered Alpha Troop to gain the initiative from an entrenched and elusive opponent. Alpha Troop's police mentoring mission revealed that CERP served broader purposes than simply building schools, wells, or roads. CERP enabled creative and resourceful officers to address an urgent humanitarian crisis. It additionally provided invaluable hands-on training for a corrupt, incompetent, and unprofessional police force. Within months, CERP-funded projects rehabilitated the ANP's tarnished reputation and improved its overall efficiency. Free from excessive bureaucratic oversight, the CERP permitted rapid, responsive, and autonomous decision-making at the tactical level. Directed by a highly motivated junior officer, the PMT's use of CERP and humanitarian assistance funds revealed that money, if used properly, could marginalize and separate an entrenched insurgency from a population.

Alpha Troop's eight-month police mentoring mission disrupted the Taliban's stranglehold on a key smuggling corridor and turned the population against a ruthless, brutal, and dedicated foe. The surge of humanitarian and medical assistance, enhanced educational opportunities, expanded police presence, and door-to-door interaction with the populace emboldened Musahi residents to push back against the Taliban. To be sure, the security gains were fragile, limited, and reversible. It remains difficult to measure the long-term effectiveness of Operations UNITED FRONT I and II in impeding the flow of weapons into Kabul or forcing insurgents to shift their bases of operations. Yet, if securing actionable intelligence from the populace about weapons caches, the identity of suspected insurgents, and the location of smuggling routes constitute legitimate performance metrics, the Soldiers of Alpha Troop succeeded in seizing the initiative from the Taliban. In this case, CERP assistance cash was a weapons system just as effective as rifles, artillery, and airpower.

Alpha Troop Soldiers marveled at their different wartime experiences in Afghanistan and Iraq. During Operation IRAQI FREEDOM, Staff Sergeant Marcello served on a brigade quick reaction force (QRF) in Al Anbar Province from 2005-2006. In conventional fighting, he recalled, "you prepped the battlefield with artillery and air support and then you go in with ground forces. [In Afghanistan,] we prepped that battlefield with earning the trust [of the population] and getting the people ... what they needed."[53] CERP proved vital in winning non-kinetic engagements. The program provided the "leeway" and autonomy for Soldiers to meet unique local needs and challenges.[54] Frey argued that CERP was the "most influential and best tool" for winning the hearts and minds of Musahi residents "ever put ... into our toolbox."[55] Not only did the program allow the PMT to respond to urgent humanitarian and reconstruction needs, it provided on-the-job training for the local ANP. The HA deliveries and door-to-door demographic surveys enabled the PMT to instruct the ANP in mounted and dismounted patrolling techniques, security perimeter placement, vehicle searches, establishing inner and outer cordons, detention procedures, filing reports, and interrogation techniques. Previously isolated on security observation posts and unwilling to engage the population, the Musahi ANP by the summer of 2011 led regular patrols, gained tactical proficiency, and interacted with valley residents. According to Frey, by the time Alpha Troop Soldiers departed Kabul, the ANP's professionalization was still in its "infancy stages," but their short-term improvements were a testament to effective mentorship and well-focused HA distributions. For the first time in the war, the Taliban's iron grip on the Musahi valley, if only temporarily, had been loosened.[56]

Notes

1. First Lieutenant Dennis Frey, Jr., e-mail to Anthony E. Carlson, Combat Studies Institute, Fort Leavenworth, KS, 4 January 2012. Lieutenant Frey's population figures, based on a 2011 census conducted by US Soldiers, are larger than the 2002 estimate of the Office of the United Nations High Commissioner for Refugees (UNHCR). See UNHCR, UNHCR Sub-Office Central Region DISTRICT PROFILE, 29 April 2002, http://www.aims.org.af/afg/dist_profiles/unhcr_district_profiles/central/kabul/mussahi.pdf (accessed 4 January 2012).

2. First Lieutenant Dennis Frey, Jr., interview by Anthony E. Carlson, Combat Studies Institute, Ft. Leavenworth, KS, 15 November, 2011, 6-7, 16; Staff Sergeant Michael D. Belleci, interview by Anthony E. Carlson, Combat Studies Institute, Ft. Leavenworth, KS, 28 November 2011, 3-5, 7-8, 19; Staff Sergeant Christopher Marcello, interview by Anthony E. Carlson, Combat Studies Institute, Ft. Leavenworth, KS, 22 November 2011, 8-10, 14-15, 25; Second Lieutenant Sean Polson, "Operation UNITED FRONT; A Focus on Musahi Valley," Task Force Fury Tribune 1 (January 2011): 11.

3. Operation UNITED FRONT I will be described in the text. For an overview of the operations, see, First Lieutenant Michael Hoffman, "Clearing the Musahi Valley," Task Force Fury Tribune 1 (May 2011): 9.

4. Dr. Donald P. Wright and Colonel Timothy R. Reese, On Point II: Transition to the New Campaign: The United States Army in Operation IRAQI FREEDOM, May 2003-January 2005 (Ft. Leavenworth, KS: Combat Studies Institute, 2008), 375; Major Jason W. Condrey, The Commander's Emergency Response Program: A Model for Future Implementation (Ft. Leavenworth, KS: School of Advanced Military Studies, 2010), 11-12

5. Wright and Reese, 375-77.

6. Wright and Reese, 33, 375-77; Condrey, 13.

7. Wright and Reese, 376-77; Special Inspector General for Afghanistan Reconstruction, Quarterly Report to the United States Congress, 30 October 2011, http://www.sigar.mil/pdf/quarterlyreports/oct2011/Lores/Oct2011Web.pdf (accessed 8 December 2011), 50.

8. Emphasis in original. Headquarters, United States Forces-Afghanistan (USFOR-A), Money as a Weapon System Afghanistan (MAAWS-A): USFOR-A Pub 1-06, Commander's Emergency Response Program (CERP) SOP (Kabul, Afghanistan: USFOR-A, 2011), 10. (Hereafter cited as MAAWS-A.)

9. Emphasis in original. MAAWS-A, 10.

10. MAAWS-A, 11.

11. MAAWS-A, 17-18.

12. Belleci, interview, 8-9, 19; Frey, interview, 33-34; Marcello, interview, 8-11, 20.

13. Quoted in Staff Sergeant Jordan Jones, "Nebraskans Involved in Successful Mission," United States National Guard, 7 February 2011, http://www.nationalguard.com/news/2011/feb/07/nebraskans-involved-in-successful-mission (accessed 9 November 2011).

14. First Lieutenant Sean Polson, interview by Anthony E. Carlson, Combat Studies Institute, Ft. Leavenworth, KS, 25 October 2011, 7-9, 17; Belleci, interview, 3-8; Marcello, interview, 15, 25; Frey, interview, 15-16.

15. Belleci, interview, 7-8, 19; Marcello, interview, 8-10; Frey, interview, 16.

16. General David H. Petraeus, COMISAF's Counterinsurgency Guidance, 27 July 2010.

17. First Lieutenant Sean Polson, e-mail to Anthony E. Carlson, Combat Studies Institute, Fort Leavenworth, KS, 19 December 2011; Frey, interview, 5-6.

18. First Lieutenant Dane Miller, e-mail to Anthony E. Carlson, Combat Studies Institute, Fort Leavenworth, KS, 12 December 2011; Marcello, interview, 19; Belleci, interview, 6-7, 31; Frey, interview, 14.

19. On the history of Afghan shuras, see Lynn Carter and Kerry Connor, *A Preliminary Investigation of Contemporary Afghan Councils* (Peshwar, Pakistan: Agency Coordinating Body for Afghan Relief, 1989), 2-10; and Ali Wardak, "Jirga – A Traditional Mechanism of Conflict Resolution in Afghanistan," United Nations Online Network in Public Administration and Finance, 2003, unpan1.un.org/intradoc/groups/public/.../apcity/unpan917434.pdf (accessed 17 August 2011).

20. Frey, interview, 35.

21. Frey, interview, 18.

22. First Lieutenant Dennis Frey, Jr., e-mail to Anthony E. Carlson, Combat Studies Institute, Fort Leavenworth, KS, 13 December 2011.

23. Frey, interview, 17-19.

24. Captain Jeremy Szynskie, interview by Anthony E. Carlson, Combat Studies Institute, Ft. Leavenworth, KS, 9 November 2011, 8-10.

25. Szynskie, interview, 16.

26. Szynskie, interview, 12-21.

27. Frey, interview, 20.

28. Frey, interview, 22.

29. Frey, interview, 22, 24; Belleci, 25-6; John David Blom, *Unmanned Aerial Systems: A Historical Perspective* (Ft. Leavenworth, KS: Combat Studies Institute, 2010), 112.

30. Belleci, interview, 28-9.

31. Staff Sergeant Chris Marcello, e-mail to Anthony E. Carlson, Combat Studies Institute, Fort Leavenworth, KS, 6 January 2012.

32. Jones, "NebraskansInvolved in Successful Mission"; Second Lieutenant Sean Polson, "Nebraska National Guardmembers [sic.] Make Inroads into Taliban Stronghold," National Guard News, 8 February 2011, http://www.ng.mil/news/archives/2011/02/020811-Nebraska.aspx (accessed 14 October 2011); Miller, e-mail, 12 December 2011.

33. Jones, "Nebraskans Involved in Successful Mission"; Polson, interview, 11-13; First Lieutenant Dennis Frey, Jr., e-mail to Anthony E. Carlson, Combat Studies Institute, Ft. Leavenworth, KS, 12 December 2011.

34. Miller, e-mail, 12 December 2011.

35. Miller, e-mail, 12 December 2011.

36. Belleci, interview, 22-23.

37. Frey, interview, 25; Jones, "Nebraskans Involved in Successful Mission."

38. Frey, interview, 39-40; Second Lieutenant Sean Polson, "Discovered Weapons Cache," Task Force Fury Tribune 1 (March 2011): 4.

39. Polson, interview, 24.

40. Polson, interview, 23-24.

41. Polson, interview, 27-28; First Lieutenant Sean Polson, "Operation UNITED FRONT II: Afghan Freedom Fighters," Task Force Fury Tribune 1 (May 2011): 4.

42. First Lieutenant Dain Miller, e-mail to Anthony E. Carlson, Combat Studies Institute, Fort Leavenworth, KS, 13 December 2011.

43. Polson, interview, 27; Polson, "Operation UNITED FRONT II"; Marcello, interview, 30.

44. Marcello, interview, 31-32; Belleci, interview, 36-37; Frey, interview, 30.

45. Frey, interview, 27-28, quote at 28.

46. Polson, "Operation UNITED FRONT II," 5; Frey, interview, 30-34.

47. Polson, "Operation UNITED FRONT II," 6.

48. UNHCR Sub-Office Central Region DISTRICT PROFILE, 2.

49. Captain Szynskie, "CPT Szynskie Top Five Projects," unpublished paper in author's possession, 3 November 2011, 1-2.

50. Captain Szynskie, e-mail to Anthony E. Carlson, Combat Studies Institute, Fort Leavenworth, KS, 14 December 2011; Frey, interview, 37-38.

51. Department of the Army, Field Manual (FM) 3-0, Operations (Headquarters, Department of the Army: Washington, DC: 2008), 3-1.

52. Emphasis in original. Department of the Army, *Field Manual (FM) 3-0*, page 3-3.

53. Marcello, interview, 35.

54. Marcello, interview, 17.

55. Frey, interview, 17.

56. Frey, interview, 42.

Partnership in Paktika Province
2010-2011

by

Ryan D. Wadle, Ph.D.

In September 2010, the people of Afghanistan prepared to take part in only the second parliamentary elections in the country's modern history. Lieutenant Colonel Donn Hill, commander, 2d Battalion, 506th Infantry Regiment (2-506 IN) – designated Task Force White Currahee - knew that election polling sites represented a rich target for insurgent forces attempting to delegitimize the Government of the Islamic Republic of Afghanistan (GIRoA). Two days before the elections, elements of Hill's battalion and their partners from the Afghan National Security Forces (ANSF) established a checkpoint in the village of Tamira approximately five kilometers from Orgun-e, the economic hub of Paktika Province. The two units worked in concert to prevent insurgents from Pakistan traveling through Paktika Province to Kabul and other major Afghan cities. This partnership helped re-establish a Coalition presence in the countryside, and, most importantly, successfully interdicted the insurgents hoping to disrupt the parliamentary elections. As Hill put it, the enemy "was pissed off, because that's how he was going to bring in a bunch of stuff to interfere with the elections. [We] totally got inside his decision cycle two days out."[1] This example of partnership allowed the elections to proceed unimpeded and set back the insurgency's attempts to influence public participation in the election.

Background

From summer 2010 until summer 2011, units of the 4th Brigade Combat Team (BCT) of the 101st Airborne Division, Air Assault – designated Task Force Currahee – worked to extend Coalition influence throughout Paktika Province in eastern Afghanistan. The deployment to Paktika included two combat battalions, including 1st Battalion, 506th Infantry Regiment (1-506 IN) – designated Red Currahee – and 2-506 IN. These two battalions received support from their brigade's 4th Brigade Special Troops Battalion (4th BSTB) which contained military police, intelligence, administration, and engineering units within a single battalion. During the year, Soldiers from the 4th BCT conducted numerous operations throughout the province, but one of their most important involved partnering with ANSF units from the Afghan National Army (ANA), Afghan Border Police (ABP), and the Afghan Uniformed Police (AUP, also known as the Afghan

National Police, or ANP). "Partnering" lacked a single, clear definition among the Soldiers tasked with implementing it. In practice, it called for American units to work closely with the ANSF to conduct operations, but also with an expectation that the Americans would mentor and train their partners. Typically, an American unit found itself partnered with at least one, if not more, unit of equivalent size from the three branches of the ANSF. In a larger context, partnership was crucial as a means to build up ANSF capabilities, a factor crucial to those military forces waging a counterinsurgency (COIN) campaign against indigenous and foreign fighters attempting to destabilize a nation. Improving the Afghans' security capabilities was also essential because the pending reduction in the number of International Security Assistance Force (ISAF) troops present in Afghanistan meant that the Afghans needed to assume more of their own security burden. Partnering between ISAF and ANSF forces aimed simultaneously to improve the security situation in Afghanistan and prepare for the day in which foreign troops would leave the country.[2]

Coalition and insurgent forces operated in Paktika Province as early as the first year of Operation ENDURING FREEDOM. In 2002, US and British forces cleared the area around Orgun-e of insurgents as part of Operation MOUNTAIN LION. Later that year, a permanent military presence was established in the province with the construction of Camp Harrimann, later renamed Forward Operating Base (FOB) Orgun-e. By 2006, the province came under the jurisdiction of Regional Command-East (RC-East) as al Qaeda and Taliban forces began using Paktika as a base of operations against the Coalition. Typically, the American presence in Paktika consisted of a single infantry battalion because US forces were spread thin throughout RC-East. In 2007, as the numbers of US troops began to increase, a second infantry battalion was added to Paktika Province. The need for two infantry battalions in Paktika remained unchanged by the time Red Currahee and White Currahee deployed to the province in summer 2010.[3]

In the campaign to bring security to the whole of Afghanistan, the location of Paktika province made it an important focal point for Coalition operations. First, the province's position in the middle of the long border between Afghanistan and Pakistan allowed it to be used by Pakistani-based insurgent networks and foreign fighters as an entry point into Afghan territory. Paktika's border location made it a potential infiltration point, but the lack of both natural resources and a large population (approximately

400,000 in a province approximately the size of New Jersey) meant that Paktika served more as a way point and staging area for insurgents attempting to reach more strategically important provinces to the north, such as Kabul, or Highway One that circled the entire country. Influence in the province was divided between its two largest cities; Sharana, in west Paktika, served as the political center of the province while Orgun-e was the economic hub. Furthermore, the province's remoteness and poverty caused GIRoA and its predecessors to place a relatively low priority on economic infrastructure development in the area.[4]

The terrain within Paktika also had a significant effect on Coalition operations. Western Paktika province, under the control of Red Currahee, was largely flat and possessed some infrastructure. As a result, the western half of the province was relatively well-connected to GIRoA governance and economic development initiatives. A north-south ridgeline running through the center of the province culturally and economically isolated the eastern half of Paktika from these positive aspects. Lieutenant Colonel Hill, commander of White Currahee and a native of Kentucky, saw many similarities between the population of east Paktika and the Appalachia region of the United States because "the people in Appalachia don't want you to care about them, they want to be left alone. Welcome to East Paktika."[5] In fact, the people of eastern Paktika did not believe themselves residents of Afghanistan but rather part of Waziristan, the Pashtun-dominated area along the border between Afghanistan and Pakistan. When questioned by a US Soldier on patrol, a resident of Paktika stated that he had visited Afghanistan before, indicating that he did not consider himself an Afghan.[6]

Paktika's strategic importance and its deficiency in natural resources made partnership vital to the Coalition's effort to extend government control. Greater unity of US and Afghan forces was viewed as a bridge from the Coalition-dominated campaigns to the assumption of security by the ANSF. Yet, partnering was a concept whose definition could change depending on who one asked, and whose implementation could be affected by any number of factors. These difficulties, however, did not diminish the importance of partnership for the US forces in Afghanistan intent on turning over the security operations to the Afghan government. This study shows how junior officers and NCOs in Task Force Currahee attempted to work with their Afghan allies to further the Coalition's goals.

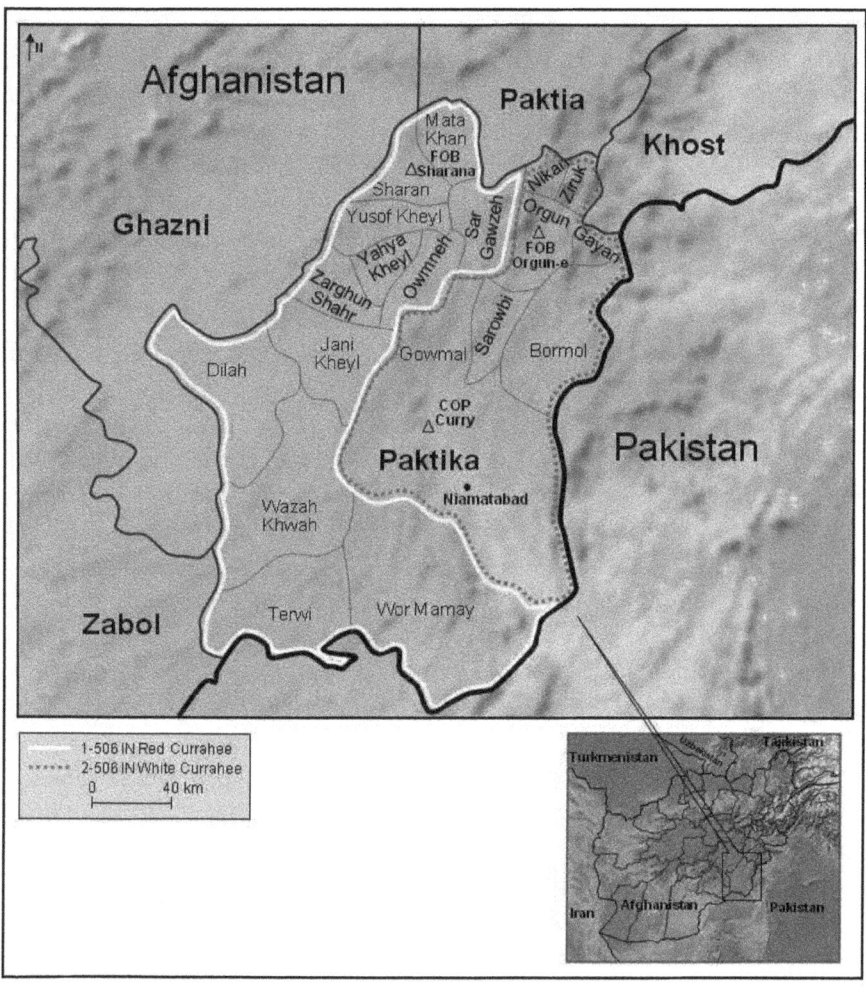

Figure 1: Map of Paktika Province.

Factors Shaping Partnerships

In interviews conducted in 2011, Soldiers from Task Force Currahee highlighted several important problems that they thought made forming effective partnerships difficult. First, Americans found that the poor training standards of ANSF units radically affected the Afghans' capabilities. Few Soldiers expected the ANSF to undergo the same costly and exhaustive training they had received, but they discovered that the ANSF troops were poorly prepared to conduct even routine patrols and other operations. Captain Jared Wagner, commander of Red Currahee's Able Company, tried to balance his belief that his battalion's desired outcome in Paktika required him to fight the enemy with the realization that the ANSF eventually needed to secure the entire country on its own. As a result, when Able Company was not conducting patrols or operations against the enemy, its Soldiers devoted their time toward informally training their ANSF partners. Unfortunately, the ANSF units in Wagner's area of operations (AO) lacked even basic knowledge of their small arms and marksmanship to say nothing of their inexperience with the tactics of patrols and other core missions. The training done by Able Company afforded Wagner and his Soldiers the opportunity to interact and bond with their ANSF counterparts, but the need to bring the Afghans up to speed in almost every basic military function limited the Americans' ability to increase the security presence in their districts.[7]

Several Soldiers also found a culture of corruption and indifference to the rule of law endemic to many elements of the ANSF. These problems undermined efforts at partnership and it interfered with attempts to persuade the residents of Paktika to accept and embrace a stronger GIRoA presence. First Lieutenant James Hyman, the 1st Platoon Leader for Easy Company, White Currahee, learned from his ANA partners that the AUP in Ziruk would charge a fee for passing though checkpoints if drivers could not produce vehicle registrations. As Hyman said, "No one in that area has a vehicle registration. They don't have DMV like we do."[8] *Staff Sergeant Billy Weiland, the platoon sergeant for 1st Platoon, Able Company, Red Currahee, noticed that members of the AUP unit he partnered with frequently went to the town bazaar to steal from the shops. He compared the situation to an American police officer "going into Best Buy or something and just taking what he wanted because he's a cop."*[9] *Such criminal activities indicated the absence of discipline and fostered mistrust and resentment among the local population.*

The rampant corruption observed in Afghanistan also denied ANSF elements the logistical support necessary to conduct effective security operations. Americans reported that Afghan Soldiers and policemen looked on the efficient supply networks of the Coalition forces with envy and often attempted to requisition supplies as a precondition for participating in operations. Afghan units did so because their own supply system functioned inconsistently and failed to provide them with even basic military necessities, leading to significant losses in confidence and morale among their Soldiers and policemen. Sergeant First Class Marco Osuna, the S4 Noncommissioned Officer in Charge (NCOIC) for the 4th BSTB, noted that the ANSF often kept close tabs on serial-numbered items such as weapons and vehicles, but ammunition, food, fuel, and any other bulk asset became fodder for corruption as those items moved through the logistical networks.[10] *Staff Sergeant Lucas Kudrna of the Headquarters* and Headquarters Company (HHC), 4th BSTB, said that if an ANSF unit ordered a thousand rounds of ammunition, "by the time it got down to the people that need it, they had a hundred rounds left."[11] By decreasing the operational effectiveness of the ANSF and straining on American logistics, the corruption in the Afghan supply network inhibited effective partnerships.

American Soldiers frequently lamented the poor leadership that plagued many of the ANSF units they partnered with. The success or failure of partnership rested on the desire of commanders on both sides to work with one another. While some American officers and NCOs found well-trained and eager partners, others reported that their counterparts were grossly incompetent, opposed to working with Americans, or some combination thereof. The ANSF had yet to evolve into a true meritocracy where officers received promotions based solely on their abilities. Instead, many officers could thank political or familial connections for their status, meaning that failure for an ANSF officer did not mean dismissal or a reduction in responsibilities.[12]

The internal hierarchy of the ANSF also indirectly contributed to the challenge of finding willing partners. Long after the end of the Soviet occupation, the Afghans still used the Soviet model for unit organization where company commanders and platoon leaders both led and executed all major directives and failed to delegate significant responsibilities to their senior NCOs. The Afghan system, intended to foster political reliability within the officer corps, differed radically from US practice in which senior NCOs carried out the orders of their commanding officers and were also expected to offer counsel to officers making important decisions. The Afghan system marginalized their senior NCOs from both decision-making and the execution of orders. First Lieutenant Joe Wright from White Currahee's Fox Company reported that when he discussed upcoming missions with his ANA counterpart, the decision to proceed rested solely in the hands of the Afghan officer without any input from his senior NCOs. Dog Company's First Lieutenant James Lee recounted that ANSF platoon leaders set the tone for the competence and aggressiveness of their units regardless of the strengths or assets that the other Soldiers or policemen brought to the table. With the Soviet system in place, the success of a partnership between entire American and ANSF units often rested on the shoulders of a very few.[13]

US Army officers sometimes found that forging closer ties with ANSF units compromised their operational security (OPSEC). Lieutenant Colonel Hill did not have a consistent ANA presence in his Tactical

Operations Center (TOC) due to strong suspicions that the Afghan Liaison and Observer (L&O) assigned to his headquarters was feeding information to the enemy. Most other concerns about OPSEC arose from the indirect transfer of information to insurgent forces. Companies assigned to partner with AUP and ABP units – those most likely to recruit personnel from Paktika – quickly learned that they could not provide much advance warning about the targets and objectives of upcoming missions for fear of the information leaking. Such leaks led to search operations sometimes referred to as "catastrophic successes" that uncovered no significant caches of weapons or suspicious military-age males. As Captain Dale Marrou, commander of Baker Company, Red Currahee, stated, "every time they knew about something more than literally 12 hours in advance, word got out and the people in whatever village we were going to when we got there said 'oh yeah, we heard you were coming, we expected you.' So of course, you didn't find anything, nothing of consequence."[14]

Some of these failures stemmed not from malice but rather information filtering through the Afghan kinship networks or casual conversations with locals. Even innocuous discussions by an Afghan soldier or policeman of his current whereabouts or future destinations could filter through the population quickly. To combat this, Soldiers from White Currahee's Weapons Company withheld the objectives of their missions until they were under way, or, in some instances, deliberately misled the Afghans about their destination until the last possible moment. As could be expected, such methods proved unworkable in the long term and created friction in the partnering relationship. Instead, Lieutenant Wright reported that Fox Company's leadership found a less polarizing solution by describing operations to their Afghan counterparts only in the vaguest of terms until the missions began. US Soldiers from Able Company, 4th BSTB, gathered all personal communications devices during mission briefs and did not return them until after completing the mission.[15]

Perhaps the biggest hindrances to forming effective partnerships were the ANSF deployment schedules. Because of eastern Paktika's ruggedness and isolation, ANSF leaders considered the area a hardship deployment and often rotated units through these districts every two or three months. Even in a poverty-stricken and war-torn country such as Afghanistan, many Afghan Soldiers and policemen found Paktika an unpleasant location. Thus, the platoons and companies of White Currahee rarely had the opportunity to build up the longer-term relationships that made partnering possible. This problem appeared in ANSF units which hailed from the Tajik- and Uzbek-dominated northern regions of Afghanistan and who found the Pashtun-dominated Paktika Province especially alien. ANSF soldiers from other parts of Afghanistan that spoke Dari also had to overcome a significant language barrier because the Pashtuns speak Pashto. Both languages are part of the Iranian language subfamily and share some similarities, but the two diverged a millennium ago and thus evolved quite differently. As a result, units comprised primarily of non-Pashtuns encountered difficulty communicating with the Paktikans and, like their American counterparts, often relied upon interpreters when patrolling. As expected, the communication barrier undercut the ANSF's ability to endear itself to Paktikans skeptical of GIRoA influence.[16]

The diverse ethnic and tribal origins of units also led to strong interservice rivalries and, at times, outbreaks of violence between the ANA, AUP, and ABP. Multiple officers and NCOs reported witnessing gunfights between ANA soldiers and AUP policemen. As Captain Hank Hansen, commander of White Currahee's Easy Company, recalled, "My first day when I came to do the relief in place (RIP) with the outgoing commander, there was a gunfight between the ANA and the AUP... just a shootout, old west style shootout where nobody gets shot."[17] While this was an extreme example of internal strife, it demonstrated the lack of cohesion within the ANSF. Such tensions resulted from ethnic strife, jealousy over perceived favoritism of one branch of the ANSF over another, and the frequent lack of clear delineation of responsibilities between the three services.

Out in the field, US soldiers sometimes found their ANSF partners unreliable in combat situations. For combat units in Paktika, typical missions involved patrolling nearby villages, clearing homes occupied by suspected insurgents of weapons and bomb-making materials, and manning checkpoints to keep Afghan roadways safe. In the Yusof Kheyl and Yahya Kheyl districts, Red Currahee's Able Company found that the ANSF proved very aggressive when they could achieve quick success against a suspected insurgent cell. On the other hand, the same units rarely wanted to conduct patrols necessary to keeping their outposts relatively safe from insurgent attack.[18] This situation only exacerbated when Able Company turned responsibility for the Yahya Kheyl outposts over to the ANSF in mid-2011. The ANSF frequently took fire on their compounds because, in Captain Wagner's analysis, they were "not alert, not attentive, not patrolling, not pulling guard."[19] First Lieutenant Daniel Stevens, 1st Platoon leader in White Currahee's Weapons Company, noted that the Afghans willingly led patrols to gain that experience, but that they showed little regard for the positions of other Soldiers when firefights erupted. Stevens recounted that when they made contact with the enemy, he always *asked his Soldiers, "'Where are you in relation to the Afghans?' Because... sometimes you just don't know what they're going to do."* [20] *The inability of the ANSF to successfully execute all of the combat roles assigned to them cast doubts on whether US Soldiers could trust them to shoulder more of the security burden.*

These obstacles certainly hampered efforts to create effective partnerships and frequently frustrated US Soldiers who worked with the Afghans regularly. In spite of these challenges, these same US Soldiers readily acknowledged that their ANSF counterparts in Pakitka brought unique skills to the table that Americans could never learn, and that these traits served as useful starting points from which to build partnerships. First and foremost, Americans singled out the hardy, adaptable nature of their Afghan partners. While 30 years of incessant war in Afghanistan has brought untold physical and psychological devastation to the Afghan people, it also infused them with a survivor's mentality that Americans found admirable. As Captain Hansen said of the Afghans, "They're just very resourceful people because they have to be. They're survivalists." [21] *Afghans often lived in more Spartan conditions than their American counterparts and received only a fraction of the training and support from their government than that expected by US Soldiers. The practical experience they had gained through three decades of war, however, often made up for these deficiencies. At times, the Afghans operated with a fearless bravado, such as when ANA Route Clearance Package (RCP) Soldiers simply fired a round from an M-16 to destroy a roadside IED rather than using the safer procedures developed by American sappers.* [22]

The other significant asset Americans found helpful in their Afghan partners was their knowledge of the country's physical and human terrain. By the time of the 4th BCT's deployment to Paktika Province in 2010, the United States had been fighting in Afghanistan for nearly 10 years. Yet, despite the US Soldiers' years of accumulated experience, they remained relative outsiders to the intricacies of Afghan life. According to Captain Marrou, the ANSF "had a very good feel for the place. And a lot of people would say, 'oh, they're lackadaisical, they're not security conscious.' But they had a pretty good feel for the way things were." [23] *In fact, the spread of information through kinship networks and informal conversations with locals worked both ways; information spreading out among ANSF units could lead to a breach in OPSEC, but information could flow into ANSF forces and provide intelligence on insurgent activities. This knowledge often had limits because US company commanders often reported that the information they received from their partners rarely contained actionable intelligence, meaning that it lacked specificity or enough factual basis to initiate immediate action. Even if this knowledge had limits, it still gave the ANSF an advantage in understanding their AO.*[24]

Partnership in Practice

When the 4th BCT deployed in the summer of 2010, it possessed two essential ingredients that gave its Soldiers a greater chance of success with partnership. First, there was a brigade-wide commitment to seeing effective partnerships created. The brigade commander, Colonel Sean Jenkins, understood the value of working with the ANSF and desired that the units under his command maintain "constant contact"[25] *with their Afghan counterparts. The brigade-wide commitment meant that multiple units often worked to solve key problems that hampered the development of partnerships. Second, many of Task Force Currahee's Soldiers had prior experience and knowledge of Paktika Province. The brigade had previously deployed there during 2008-2009, and more than half the Soldiers continued to serve in Task Force Currahee by 2010. Obviously, knowledge of the physical and human terrain was vital to the COIN campaign, but this knowledge also gave the Soldiers some prior working knowledge of the ANSF units that they expected to work with.* [26]

No discussion of partnerships between US and ANSF forces a decade after the fall of the Taliban could escape mention of the phrase "Afghan right" or "Afghan good." Soldiers at all levels recognized the unlikelihood that the ANSF could meet or surpass the level of operational effectiveness attained by the US and other military forces deployed to Afghanistan. The Americans recognized that they and the Afghans differed on what standards needed to be met to effectively secure the country. In the estimation of the US Soldiers in Paktika, many of the units they initially partnered with were not up to the "Afghan good" standard. Instead, many believed that improving the ANSF to the level of "Afghan good" would still allow the Afghans to secure their own country even if some problems persisted. For instance, Americans could tolerate some corruption, such as Afghan Soldiers and policemen taking tolls at checkpoints from passersby, so long as it remained on the margins and had no effect the Coalition's larger mission goals.[27] *Obviously, the danger of this approach was that the Coalition could potentially sacrifice long-term stability for short-term security. This process of cultural compromise, however, allowed the Afghans to discover their own solutions to problems plaguing their nascent nation.*

If partnership's ultimate goal was to improve the ANSF so that its units could eventually assume the security burden, then US units felt obligated to eliminate the ANSF's deficiencies. Members of the 4th

BSTB stationed at FOB Sharana worked to improve the administrative capabilities of their ANSF counterparts. First Lieutenant Ron Keplinger, the S1 Personnel Officer, partnered with several AUP officers in charge of finances and various aspects of personnel administration. Keplinger found that his partners had previously performed administration duties without the help of computers and instead haphazardly maintained written records. First Lieutenant Heidi Dailey, the battalion's S6 Communications Officer, set about improving the ANSF's communications systems and training their personnel how to use them. Dailey believed that while Afghans adapted quite easily to different combat situations, they had little previous experience in building and maintaining an efficient communications system. Surprisingly, Dailey detected virtually no hostility from her partners because of her gender, and she quickly endeared himself to the Afghans by informally learning Pashto and becoming somewhat fluent in the language by the end of her deployment. Because of the combined efforts of Keplinger and Dailey, their Afghan partners had a rudimentary internet system called MOI-Net up and running by spring 2011, and their personnel began to quickly adapt to the new system and more efficient methods of administration.[28]

The best partnerships in Paktika occurred when American and Afghan units forged close ties, both on and off duty. To bridge the cultural gulf between Americans and Afghans, time and patience became prized qualities. As Major Tim Hoch, the S3 of the 4th BSTB observed, "95 percent of partnership is giving a s---." Indeed, the Soldiers of the 4th BSTB's RCP took this to heart. The RCP's mission in Afghanistan was to keep the roadways in Paktika clear of Improved Explosive Devices (IEDs) using specialized vehicles and equipment. For the first several months of their deployment, the American RCP worked to clear the roads in western Paktika province. Beginning in January 2011, the RCP began partnering with an ANA company fresh from basic training in Kabul with the intent of building an equivalent route clearance capability in the ANA from scratch. Given the constant threat posed by insurgents placing IEDs along Afghan roadways, the ANA needed its own ability to clear Afghanistan's road network and keep lines of communication open.[29]

First, the American RCP made significant preparations in advance of their partners' arrival. The American RCP had sent a small team to Kabul to meet the ANA personnel before their relocation to FOB Sharana and learned their partners' strengths and weaknesses. Through these meetings, the American RCP learned that their ANA counterparts had an experienced core of officers and NCOs, but most of its personnel lacked experience with this particular mission. Captain Mark Gillman, the commander of

Able Company (Sappers), 4th BSTB, which included the RCP, studied past partnership experiences to determine the strengths and weaknesses of previous approaches. He determined that a one-to-one relationship would be crucial to avoiding problems such as desertion because past situations where ANSF units outnumbered the Americans caused the Afghan units not consistently partnered with to quickly become ineffective. The incoming ANA company had three platoons, but Gillman only had two organic route-clearance platoons at his disposal. So that both companies had the same number of platoons and to ensure a one-to-one pairing, Gillman persuaded his superiors to relocate a US Army National Guard route-clearance platoon to Sharana. ANA soldiers occasionally went AWOL over the next several months, but the desertion rate remained quite low and never adversely affected the operational effectiveness of the three ANA RCP platoons. The American Sappers regarded their ANA partners' sustainment of manpower strength as a significant accomplishment.[30]

Gillman encouraged his subordinates to partner with the ANA and to not view partnership as an unnecessary chore. Gillman's enthusiasm filtered down to his subordinates. Platoon leader First Lieutenant Bryan Bogenschutz found several ways to make his partnership with a new ANA route clearance unit successful. First, he took steps to establish a friendly relationship with his counterparts by hosting a barbecue for US and ANA Soldiers within the first week of their arrival. This simple gesture fostered goodwill between the Americans and the Afghans, and it opened up a tradition of shared meals that recurred throughout the rest of the BSTB's deployment. Next, the two units also met frequently during off-duty hours to play sports, including American-rules football and volleyball, or "wally-ball" as the Afghans pronounced it.[31]

This investment of off-duty time certainly helped create an atmosphere conducive to effective partnership, but Bogenschutz found other means of improving the relationship between the two units. Soon after the partnership began, he created a "face book" that showed pictures and names of each Afghan Soldier in the ANA route clearance platoon and circulated copies to everyone in the American RCP. This book also included photos of each Afghan Soldier in uniform manning his designated post in their vehicles so that US Soldiers could associate an Afghan with a particular position or task when preparing for or conducting operations. Memorizing this information made it easier for the Americans to quickly identify their counterparts and helped build a greater sense of trust between the two units.[32]

The efforts made by Gillman and Bogenschutz paid off handsomely over the course of their deployment. The ANA route-clearance unit made dramatic improvements in its operational effectiveness during the four months that they partnered with Gillman's men. By April, the ANA RCP began conducting security patrols without US assistance and, by all accounts, worked successfully to diminish the IED threat in western Paktika province. As Bogenschutz said, "it got to the point when we wouldn't even have to go out with them.... They said, 'You know, we got this one.' We're like, 'OK'. They'd go out and, they'd find something, they'd disable it, or they'd bring [an IED] back and we would take care of it." The ANA still needed some of the equipment that Americans deemed essential for engineering work, particularly demolition explosives, but their eagerness to assume more of the operational burden signaled that the partnership had proven fruitful in establishing an entire new ANA mission capability.[33]

Figure 2: Weekly team building dinner for the US and ANA RCPs at FOB Sharana, 27 February 2011.

Photo courtesy of Captain Mark Gillman

One recurring challenge was ensuring that gains made while US and ANSF units worked together carried over once the deployments ended. Again, the unit rotations hampered the ability of American Soldiers to establish good working relationships with their ANSF partners. New units brought new commanders with different styles and mission priorities, and the relationships often needed to be rebuilt from scratch. The RCP, however, took steps to ensure that whatever gains made by the ANA during their six months together would stick. During the final weeks of his deployment, Bogenschutz worked to introduce his successor to his ANA counterparts in order to breed familiarity and trust between them so that the professional, if not the personal, partnership could continue.[34]

The MP platoon attached to the HHC, 4th BSTB, also worked directly and indirectly to improve the partnering relationship between American units and the AUP. When the MPs first arrived in the summer of 2010, their initial duties included partnering with an AUP unit, but, after a few months, circumstances forced a change in the MP's mission. Observations made by Soldiers in the field suggested that the quality of AUP units assigned to the different district police stations in Paktika varied widely both in the amount of training and standards of discipline. Also, in many areas, the AUP functioned as a paramilitary organization and an adjunct to the ANA rather than one devoted to policing and security missions. As a result, AUP officers often had a rudimentary understanding of military tactics but knew little of policing methods. These problems were confirmed when a survey conducted among the residents of Paktika uncovered extremely high dissatisfaction with the AUP detachments.[35]

Prior to the MP's arrival, US contractors trained the AUP in Paktika with varying degrees of success. The combined effect of the negative reports on the AUP led the brigade leadership to employ the MP platoon to solve this problem. To carry out this mission, the MPs established the Currahee Focused Police District Mentoring Program (CFPDM) in September 2010. Much like the RCP's work with the ANA, the MPs attempted to tailor the training program based on specific deficiencies in the AUP units. The first step of the program involved US Soldiers observing and partnering with AUP units to determine what areas of training needed to be emphasized. Then, the bulk of the AUP from a district center – usually numbering between 30 and 60 policemen – would rotate to FOB Sharana in western Paktika Province to begin the training cycle.[36]

Under normal circumstances, moving such large numbers of policemen out of their districts could have caused significant security risks, but two developments made the transfer possible. First, the CFPDM began in September 2010 just as the fighting season came to a close. The harsh winters and rugged terrain made fighting difficult and often led to protracted lulls in insurgent attacks. For the Coalition, winter presented an ideal period to conduct extended training and to refit Afghan personnel for the next fighting season. Second, the first group of graduates from the CFPDM rotated to fill any gaps at a district police station while the local personnel trained at Sharana which minimized the impact of the transfers. This first group, known as the Shaheen (Eagles), numbered 80 policemen and was the largest class ever admitted into the program. Once the MPs completed training one AUP unit, the policemen returned to their station and the Shaheen moved on to the next district in the training rotation. The Shaheen's numbers gradually fell to approximately 25 policemen due to attrition and desertion by mid-2011, but the group continued to function as the replacement unit for the entirety of the CFPDM's existence.[37]

First Lieutenant Michael Rasmusson, the MP Platoon Leader, insisted that the CFPDM's training regimens allowed the AUP to "crawl, walk, [and then] run."[38] *One of the first priorities was to bring the AUP up to speed on law enforcement. Instead of enforcing the laws passed by Afghanistan's National Assembly, AUP units often enforced the unwritten mandates passed down by local shura councils that allowed locals to meet informally and negotiate solutions to their problems. The MPs tried to break the AUP of the habit of deferring to local pressures when performing their duties. In many areas, the AUP had been observed bending their responsibilities at the whim of either local citizens or prominent leaders. Both of these issues often led to the inconsistent enforcement of law from district to district.*[39]

As the training progressed, the MPs attempted to address each of the AUP's shortcomings and bring them up to a uniform standard. This included training on standards and discipline to make the AUP more distinct and easily recognizable to the local populace, tactical training that kept officers safe while appearing non-threatening to citizens, and learning policing skills. Some of this training occurred in the classroom, but the MPs also included scenario-based training to give more of a hands-on approach, including one exercise where they sent their students out to the local bazaar and recorded their interactions with the public for later critiquing. To keep the trainees stimulated, the instructors interspersed classroom sessions with exercises throughout the day. The trainees took to the program well, especially because many enjoyed the respite that the CFPDM provided from the relative isolation and danger that they faced in their districts.[40]

The CFPDM worked extremely well during the winter months, and those who interacted with the program's graduates were pleased with the results. American officers who partnered with CFPDM graduates witnessed a noticeable uptick in their effectiveness and discipline. Lieutenant Hyman from Easy Company said of the graduates that, "I think they knew their job better and I think the biggest thing was an understanding of the ethics that were expected out of them. I think that training was valuable because before that I don't think they really understood what was expected of them."[41] The Soldiers of Red Currahee's Able Company successfully used CFPDM graduates to create an informal special reaction team (SRT) capable of conducting aggressive search and clearing operations.[42] Sergeant Kudrna noted that the graduates of the program itself realized it had improved their skills, and, as a result, graduates who passed through FOB Sharana on official business for their district stopped at the training center to greet and thank the trainers. The public also noticed a difference in the AUP after they completed the training. Locals related to Kudrna that, "These guys are polite. They don't yell at kids, they're not mean to women, they're not mean to people – they're actually out saying hello, talking to shopkeepers, getting involved."[43]

Unfortunately, not every American unit partnered with the AUP could benefit from the CFPDM. Captain John Rascher, the commander of India Company, White Currahee, recalled that he needed air assets to move large numbers of men in and out of his AO in Gowmal District. With helicopter transportation stretched thin throughout Afghanistan, any AUP unit that left for training often had to wait some time before getting transportation back to Gowmal. Additionally, the Afghan policemen believed that rotation out of Gowmal entitled them to take leave back to their homes and families. As Rascher described, "So we'd get them to a school, and they wouldn't come back for months, if at all."[44] In this case, the need for a consistent security presence in Gowmal outweighed any potential benefits the AUP might have received from the CFPDM.

The CFPDM proved short-lived because the warming weather of spring 2011 signaled the start of a new fighting season. A rise in the number of potential insurgent attacks made local district chiefs reluctant to part with so many policemen at one time. As a result of this feedback, the MPs adapted the CFPDM into a new training program named Ten for Ten. As its name indicated, ten AUP officers received a condensed version of the CFPDM training in both classroom and scenario-based training over a period of ten days. Ten for Ten tried to compromise between the intensive training of the older program with reduced numbers of men taken from *each police district and the length of the training period to address the concerns of the district chiefs. The Ten for Ten program remained in place for the remainder of the MPs deployment and proved a successful compromise in balancing the need for additional training with the security situation in the province.*[45]

All of the successes achieved by the 4th BSTB's RCP, staff, and MPs in helping to establish new capabilities within the ANSF and enhancing partnerships throughout Paktika occurred at FOB Sharana, the province's administrative center. While Soldiers at Sharana faced serious dangers – a pair of suicide bombers attacked the police headquarters at the FOB in November 2010 and killed a dozen Afghan policemen – and the corruption and dysfunction common in Afghan institutions, the situation at Sharana was far more secure than that faced by infantry companies and platoons in the smaller outposts scattered throughout Paktika.[46] *At these posts, some of which saw daily contact with the enemy, forming effective partnerships became even more difficult because some of the techniques did not easily carry over to platoons partnered in isolated COPs. For instance, the need for security in the more contested areas prevented American officers and NCOs from traveling to meet their new partners as the US RCP did. The lack of proper facilities inhibited Americans from subjecting their ANSF partners to the same rigorous training and mentoring that Afghans at Sharana received. Additionally, American Soldiers found that the short overlaps between deployments cut down on the amount of time available to get to know their ANSF partners and made it difficult to bridge relationships. According to Captain Marrou:*

> *You know in a ten-day RIP (Relief in Place) process, the unit coming in, in addition to having to sign for a property book which was twice the size of a property book you have back in the rear, and he's got to do all that in ten days, and, oh, by the way, you'd better make sure your shortage annexes are straight and all this other crap, well, then he's also got to try and learn a little bit of something about the AO. And learn about the personalities, and that's ten days. It's a fire hose effect to the umpteenth.*[47]

With these hurried timetables, American Soldiers could only devote a small portion of their time to meeting their partners during these brief and hectic rotations.

In spite of all of these constraints, however, combat units still found ways to bond with the ANSF. White Currahee's Weapons Company, for example, found its ANSF partners difficult to work with early in their deployment. Sergeant First Class William Allen thought the Afghans deliberately underplayed their own capabilities in order to shift more of the operational burden onto the Americans. Even worse, US Soldiers discovered the Afghans stealing their personal property from the joint TOC, and the ANSF leadership virtually ignored the accusations made by the Americans. After some heated exchanges, the Americans and Afghans began operating out of separate TOCs, but the separation allowed the relationship to mend and flourish. The US and ANA Soldiers began working on a driver's education program that many Afghans completed, and the planning and coordination of operations also improved dramatically. In fact, Weapons Company's 3d Platoon became informally attached to an ABP platoon and began operating together frequently because the two units began trusting one another. While members of the Weapons Company believed that their partners still needed improvements to function more efficiently and effectively, they had successfully overcome a rocky beginning. [48]

Many Americans discovered that simply conducting business with their ANSF partners in a more relaxed, informal way often won the Afghans over. American Soldiers prided themselves on the efficiency and briskness with which they conducted their business, but they learned that Afghans interpreted such behavior, particularly with strangers, as curt and rude. Based on personal experience and knowledge of Afghan culture, some Americans achieved positive results by altering their approach to personal interactions. Lieutenant Hyman from White Currahee's Easy Company built up his relationship with his AUP partner by listening to the police chief's stories about his service in the mujahedeen under Ahmed Shah Masoud during the Soviet occupation. At some point during their interactions, Hyman's counterpart would ask what he could do for Hyman, indicating that the altered approach yielded success. Hyman's company commander, Captain Hansen, also learned through his personal experience that "getting officers and senior NCOs to be involved with [the Afghans], sit, drink and have chai and try to get to know them better I think is one of the best things to do."[49] Building up these personal ties eventually gave Hansen more leeway in demanding greater accountability from his ANSF partners.[50]

Other officers in Paktika used their relationships with ANSF partners for multiple positive endeavors. Lieutenant Sean Peloquin, 1st Platoon leader in Red Currahee's Baker Company, got to know his AUP partner through regular conversations over chai, watching TV together (even though Peloquin found local programming incomprehensible), and eating dinner together at least twice a week. These interactions sometimes *involved Peloquin's entire platoon, and this bond allowed the American to improve their partner's effectiveness. Thanks to the solid rapport between Peloquin and his AUP partner, their combined efforts allowed the AUP and the sub-governor in Mata Khan District to begin coordinating their activities for the first time. Peloquin also initiated a cross-training program with his AUP partners whereby the US and AUP units learned each other's tactics. His partner proved extremely capable and, over the course of Peloquin's deployment, the AUP began collecting intelligence and leading joint US-AUP operations in the district.*[51]

India Company's Captain Rascher likewise learned that getting to know his Afghan partners through personal interactions yielded large operational benefits. When Rascher and his Soldiers first arrived in Gowmal District, they found the Afghan Border Patrol contingent charged with guarding the Pakistan border operated out of COP Curry, nearly 50 kilometers from the border. Making matters worse, the ABP conducted patrols only with great reluctance because they lacked reliable vehicles. Eventually, the time that the Soldiers of India Company invested in their relationship, combined with the timely transfer of some HMMWVs from US to ABP control, led to a dramatic increase in the effectiveness of the ABP. In late April 2011, Soldiers from India and Whiskey Companies participated in Operation DRAGOON in which the Americans helped the ABP create a new checkpoint only 20 kilometers from the border in the village of Niamatabad (see Figure 1). Once the ABP unit established itself, the Americans returned to their COPs and the new checkpoint became the sole responsibility of the Afghans. The ABP also became self-sufficient and staged its own supply runs to and from COP Curry.[52] *As Rascher said of his ABP partners, "When they saw that we were willing to help them out, they became a lot more willing to lead from the front, and a lot quicker to acknowledge that it was their country, and their job. And some of their officers would say, you know, in front of the others, 'We should be the ones in the front, the Americans should be behind us.'"*[53]

Conclusions

The deployment of Task Force Currahee to Paktika Province in summer 2010 brought its staffs, companies, and platoons into a variety of different settings and each with its own mission to perform. These units faced the challenges of partnership with ineffective ANSF units limited by poor training, cultural and institutional rivalries, deficiencies in leadership and organization, corruption, and poor logistics. Among the components of the ANSF, only the ABP received regular praise from their American partners, while opinions of the ANA and AUP fluctuated wildly and indicated massive inconsistency in the quality of those units. The poor quality of the ANSF units meant that a wide gulf persisted between the capabilities of Afghan and American units. In a COIN campaign such as the one waged in Afghanistan, the absence of competent indigenous forces could negatively affect the Coalition war effort.

In spite of those high stakes and immense challenges, the Soldiers of Task Force Currahee found paths to forging successful partnerships with the ANSF. For many junior officers and NCOs within Task Force Currahee, training up their ANSF partners, either formally or informally, proved very successful. Many Soldiers noted that the ANSF lacked even the most basic of training when they arrived in Paktika. Without adequate training of the ANSF, American officers and NCOs could not rely upon their partners to carry their weight and perform the missions required of them. Informal programs in everything from marksmanship to driving implemented at the COPs and FOBs introduced essential skills to the ANSF. Meanwhile, the CFPDM and its successor program Ten for Ten brought about a noticeable increase in the skill-sets possessed by the AUP. Training had a multiplicative effect because the better-trained units not only learned to perform missions better but also became more cohesive and disciplined in the process. The training process itself bonded the ANSF Soldiers and policemen to each other and their American trainers, and vastly improved the chances of successful joint operations, such as the effort by White Currahee Soldiers and the ANSF to prevent disruption of the 2010 elections.

The integrated nature of the brigade's approach to partnership merits mention. Throughout Task Force Currahee's deployment, Soldiers from both combat and noncombat units of the brigade worked to remove the obstacles to successful partnership. For instance, the implementation of the CFPDM by the MPs at FOB Sharana helped remedy the deficiencies of the Afghan police force. Similarly, combat units deployed to smaller outposts likewise sought to train up their partners and improve their effectiveness. The BSTB staff officers partnered with Afghans worked to improve the creaky and dysfunctional logistical network that hampered the operational effectiveness of many ANSF units in Paktika, although the observations made by American Soldiers in the field suggests that much more needed to be done in this area. This integrated effort demonstrated the brigade's commitment to partnership and the willingness to devise multiple solutions to eliminate common shortcomings found in Afghan units.

Finally, the common link between all of the successful partnerships established between Task Force Currahee and the ANSF in Paktika involved frequent one-on-one interaction between Soldiers and policemen from different nations. Regardless of whether these relationships formed through training programs or in the field during operations, some of the best partnership successes came about through shared experiences and forging closer ties. American Soldiers accepted the different culture and expectations of their partners and modified their own conduct to suit the more relaxed and informal ways of the Afghans. Conversations over chai, shared meals, athletics, or even watching television together during off-duty hours brought Americans and Afghans closer together. In at least one case, a Soldier learning one of Afghanistan's major languages broke through the cultural barrier. Sometimes, as in the case of 3d Platoon from White Currahee's Weapons Company, the US and ANSF forged closer ties through repeated joint operations. By building up these relationships, the Americans showed more concern for the Afghan effort against the destabilizing forces of the insurgency and the Afghans responded favorably to these overtures.

Lieutenant Colonel David Womack, commander of Red Currahee, told his commanders that because of the hard work involved, "partnership, if done right, should hurt very much."[54] Womack's observation rings true as the best examples of partnership resulted from strenuous efforts by both American and Afghans to work with one another. To the credit of the US Soldiers in Paktika during 2010 and 2011, they viewed "Afghan good" as the minimum acceptable standard and often successfully trained their partners to conduct complex operations. The time and resource investment in partnering was considerable, but the payoffs, such as the joint operation preventing disruption of the 2010 elections, were incalculable.

Notes

1. Lieutenant Colonel Donn Hill, interview by Ryan Wadle, Combat Studies Institute, Fort Leavenworth, KS, 16 November 2011, 7-8.

2. Seth G. Jones, *Counterinsurgency in Afghanistan* (Arlington, VA: RAND Corporation, 2008). http://www.rand.

org/content/dam/rand/pubs/monographs/2008/RAND_MG595.pdf [accessed 11 January 2012], 15-8.

3. Donald P. Wright, James R. Bird, Steven E. Clay, Peter W. Connors, Lieutenant Colonel (LTC) Scott C. Farquhar, Lynne Chandler Garcia, and Dennis F. Van Wey, *A Different Kind of War: The United States Army in Operation ENDURING FREEDOM (OEF), October 2001-September 2005* (Ft. Leavenworth: Combat Studies Institute, 2010), 185, 216.

4. Hill, interview (Wadle), passim; Islamic Republic of Afghanistan Central Statistics Organization, *Statistical Yearbook, 2009-2010,* http://cso.gov.af/Content/files/Population.pdf [accessed 11 January 2012], p. 5.

5. Lieutenant Colonel Donn Hill, interview by Ginger Shaw, Center for Military History, Fort McNair, Washington, DC, 24 June 2011, 23.

6. Hill, interview (Shaw), 24-5.

7. Able Company, 1-506 IN (Air Assault), group interview by Ryan Wadle, Combat Studies Institute, Fort Leavenworth, KS, 16 November 2011, 13-4.

8. First Lieutenant James Hyman, quoted in Easy Company, 2-506 IN (Air Assault), group interview by Ryan Wadle, Combat Studies Institute, Fort Leavenworth, KS, 16 November 2011, 13.

9. Staff Sergeant Billy Weiland, quoted in A/1-506, group interview, 46.

10. Staff, 4th Brigade Special Troops Battalion, group interview by Ryan Wadle, Combat Studies Institute, Fort Leavenworth, KS, 17 November 2011, 17.

11. Staff Sergeant Lucas Kudrna, quoted in Headquarters and Headquarters Company, 4th Brigade Special Troops Battalion, group interview by Ryan Wadle, Combat Studies Institute, Fort Leavenworth, KS, 16 November 2011, 5.

12. A/1-506, group interview, 13-5, 25; Baker Company, 1-506 IN (Air Assault), group interview by Ryan Wadle, Combat Studies Institute, Fort Leavenworth, KS, 17 November 2011, 15-6; E/2-506, group interview, 24.

13. HHC/4th BSTB, group interview, 10; India Company, 2-506 IN (Air Assault), group interview by Ryan Wadle, Combat Studies Institute, Fort Leavenworth, KS, 17 November 2011, 11-3.

14. Captain Dale Marrou, quoted in B/1-506, group interview by Ryan Wadle, Combat Studies Institute, Fort Leavenworth, KS, 17 November 2011, 16. E/2-506, group interview, 14.

15. Weapons Company, 2-506 IN (Air Assault), group interview by Ryan Wadle, Combat Studies Institute, Fort Leavenworth, KS, 17 November 2011, 25-7; I/2-506, group interview, 25-6; Route Clearance Package, Able Company, 4th Brigade Special Troops Battalion, group interview by Ryan Wadle, Combat Studies Institute, Fort Leavenworth, KS, 18 November 2011, 30-1.

16. E/2-506, group interview, 32-3; W/2-506, group interview, 10-1.

17. Captain Hank Hansen, quoted in E/2-506, group interview, 33.

18. Captain Jared Wagner, quoted in A/1-506, group interview, 17-8.

19. Captain Jared Wagner, quoted in A/1-506, group interview, 19.

20. First Lieutenant Daniel Stevens, quoted in W/2-506, group interview, 10.

21. Captain Hank Hansen, quoted in E/2-506, group interview, 27.

22. RCP/A/4th BSTB, group interview, 9, 28.

23. Marrou, quoted in B/1-506, group interview, 31.

24. A/1-506, group interview, 20.

25. Colonel Sean Jenkins, interview by Ginger Shaw, Center for Military History, Fort McNair, Washington, DC, 24 June 2011, 17.

26. Jenkins, interview, 13-8.

27. Hill, interview (Shaw), 43-4; Lieutenant Colonel David Womack, interview by Ginger Shaw, Center for Military History, Fort McNair, Washington, DC, 23 June 2011, 8.

28. 4th BSTB Staff, group interview, 3-6, 8-9, 11-2, 36-7.

29. RCP/A/4th BSTB, group interview, 20.

30. RCP/A/4th BSTB, group interview, 10-2.

31. RCP/A/4th BSTB, group interview, 12, 24.

32. RCP/A/4th BSTB, group interview, 19, 22

33. RCP/A/4th BSTB, group interview, Quote on 35.

34. RCP/A/4th BSTB, group interview, 31-6.

35. HHC/4th BSTB, group interview, 1-3.

36. HHC/4th BSTB, group interview, 1.

37. HHC/4th BSTB, group interview, 1-3, 14-5; Lieutenant Colonel Ivan Beckman, interview by Ginger Shaw, Center for Military History, Fort McNair, Washington, DC, 22 June 2011, 17; First Lieutenant Michael Rasmusson, telephone conversation, Ryan Wadle, Combat Studies Institute, Fort Leavenworth, KS, 12 January 2012.

38. Rasmusson, quoted in HHC/4th BSTB, group interview, 3.

39. HHC/4th BSTB, group interview, 4.

40. HHC/4th BSTB, group interview, 9-13

41. Hyman, quoted in E/2-506, group interview, 9.

42. A/1-506, group interview, 43-4.

43. Kudrna, quoted in HHC/4th BSTB, group interview, 24.

44. Captain John Rascher, quoted in I/2-506, group interview, 20.

45. HHC/4th BSTB, group interview, 14-5.

46. Indo-Asian News Service, "Suicide bombers storm police HQ, kill 12," Hindustan Times, 27 November 2010, http://www.hindustantimes.com/world-news/Afghanistan/Suicide-bombers-storm-police-HQ-kill-12/Article1-631653.aspx (accessed 30 December 2011).

47. B/1-506, group interview, 41.

48. W/2-506, group interview, 4-7.

49. Hansen, quoted in E/2-506, group interview, 22.

50. E/2-506, group interview, 21.

51. B/1-506, group interview, 17-8, 31-3.

52. I/2-506, group interview, 17-20.

53. Rascher, quoted in I/2-506, group interview, 19.

54. Womack, interview, 4.

Leading the Charge
A Cavalry Platoon's Fight in Badghis Province
by
Matt M. Matthews

Early signs of spring brought little relief to Red Platoon. Led by First Lieutenant Joseph C. Law, the unit was formally designated 1st Platoon, Bravo Troop, 7th Squadron, 10th Cavalry Regiment (1/B/7-10 CAV) of the US Army's 1st Brigade Combat Team (1BCT), 4th Infantry Division (4ID). Throughout the blistering summer of 2010 and the frigid winter of 2010-11, Red Platoon had relentlessly conducted combat missions in northern Murghab District, Badghis Province, in northwest Afghanistan. For Law's platoon, operations intensified in April 2011, as they expanded security in northern Murghab. On 4 April, the platoon's Soldiers experienced the most intense firefight of their entire tour.[1]

Background

Lieutenant Colonel C. Scott Mitchell's 7-10 CAV arrived in Afghanistan in the summer of 2010. Tasked with providing security to two provinces with only 513 Soldiers, his Alpha, Charlie, Delta, Headquarters and Headquarters Troops (HHT) occupied positions in Herat Province. Bravo Troop (christened Bulldog Troop) established positions in Badghis Province. By occupying the Bala Murghab Valley in the Murghab District, Bulldog Troop was isolated from the rest of the Squadron, a situation that created a formidable logistical challenge. "The way that they received supplies primarily was by CDS (Container Delivery System) drop," Major Jonathan Lauer, the Squadron Operations Officer (S3) pointed out. "They would get two or three CDS drops a week," he explained, most of which were dropped by United States Air Force C-17 Globemaster IIIs. Lauer recalled that it took "a significant amount of effort just to keep them re-supplied up there [because] there was no secured, reliable ground route... up to Bala Murghab at all." Law also described the situation as "a logistical nightmare."[2]

Command and Control (C2) also presented challenges for 7-10 CAV. In Herat Province, units from 7-10 CAV colocated with a Spanish Task Force, while the Bulldog Troop Headquarters in Badghis Province colocated with an Italian army regiment located in the town of Bala Murghab on Forward Operating Base (FOB) Todd. "We fell in on what was a very, very complex C2 structure," Lauer emphasized. While 7-10 CAV still belonged to 1BCT, 4ID, stationed in Kandahar, they conducted operations on territory assigned to the Italian and Spanish armies. Furthermore, while both the Italians and the Spanish forces fell under Regional Command-West (RC-West), 7-10 CAV did not. The thorny C2 situation created significant tension between 7-10 CAV and its NATO allies. [3]

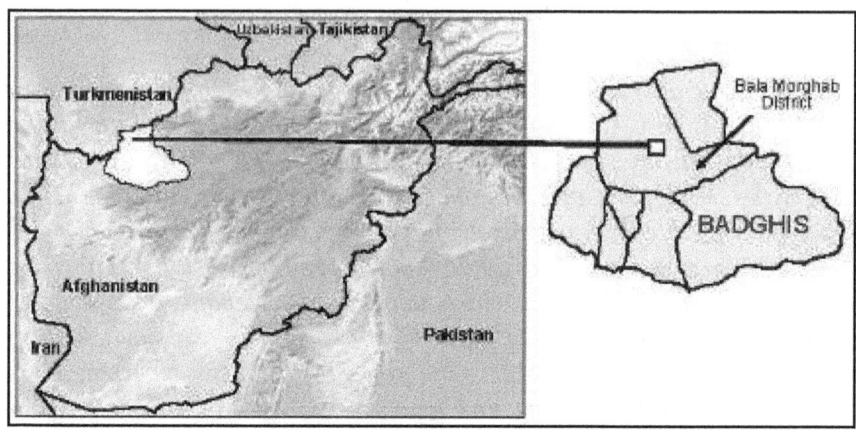

Figure 1. Badghis Province and Bala Morghab District.

Conflicting national rules of engagement (ROE) worsened the tense relationship between 7-10 CAV and its Italian and Spanish allies. "They were not prosecuting the war, necessarily, to the degree that it really demanded out there," Lauer declared. Indeed, Italian and Spanish units, along with their Afghan counterparts, performed few patrols or operations into suspected Taliban locations. "Because the Italians and Spanish didn't go [to] a lot of places, didn't actively patrol a lot of places...there was a lot of area that was relatively ungoverned, or under what was fully acknowledged to be [under] Taliban control. So there were areas you just didn't go," Lauer noted.[4]

By late March 2011, Bravo Troop, commanded by Captain Tyrek Swaby, occupied FOB Todd in the town of Bala Murghab. At the same time, Swaby's 2d Platoon (White Platoon), commanded by First Lieutenant Nick Costello, occupied a Combat Outpost (COP) south of Bala Murghab.[5] *Law's Red Platoon and an Afghan National Army (ANA) platoon manned COP Metro north of the town. All three positions were within what was referred to as the security bubble. "That bubble was really the village of Bala Murghab...our cav[alry] platoon on the north side and our cav[alry] platoon on the south side, were sort of the northern and southern boundaries of that security bubble," Lauer stated. The Squadron Operations Officer also pointed out that areas outside the security bubble were impenetrable. "If you [ventured outside the bubble] you were guaranteed to get into a fight," Lauer explained. He then referred to the large number of improvised* explosive devices (IEDs) in the area, stating, "It was heavily IEDed to the north and south. Inside the security bubble, it was relatively secure."[6]

Law bluntly decried the security situation around COP Metro. "It was trench warfare is what it was," he stated. "They were set up [north of Bala Murghab] in the valley...it was no man's land pretty much. And anybody that went up there was going to be shot at. Any kind of...coalition forces, or anything that represented the government, was going to get shot at." While there were brief lulls, the Taliban attacked Law's Platoon almost every day with small arms fire. Red Platoon regularly encountered Taliban insurgents planting IEDs. Law's Soldiers also faced a dedicated, entrenched and well-supplied enemy.[7]

With the approaching spring and improved weather conditions, 7-10 CAV intended to bolster counterinsurgency operations. "What we really wanted to do is start to connect the Afghan provincial and district governance with more...of its population," Lauer explained. In order to carry out this ambitious mission, Bulldog Troop needed to make contact with the small villages north and south of FOB TODD. The Squadron anticipated a fierce fight since improved weather also brought increased enemy activity. Soon however, White Platoon found success in the south. In what was described as a series "of fortuitous events," the platoon killed 8 to 12 Taliban fighters using a combination of close air support (CAS), and direct and indirect fire. The 7-10 CAV staff also indentified two distinct Taliban cells, one operating in the south and the other in the north.[8]

White Platoon's actions proved so successful they stood up new, temporary positions, conducted a series of patrols designed to upset enemy operations, and reestablished coalition control south of FOB TODD. "We were having a good deal of success in the south," Lauer stated, so "we wanted to try to apply that pressure to that Taliban zone in the north, because we did get a lot of indications that those two cells were working together, asking each other for help." The squadron determined to keep the enemy on its heels and pressed Bulldog Troop to conduct an operation north of COP Metro. The mission took Red Platoon further north than coalition forces had ventured since the 2001 US invasion of Afghanistan.[9]

Planning the Mission

First Lieutenant Law, a native of Moultrie, Georgia, had served three years in the US Army as an enlisted military intelligence specialist. Upon completing his enlistment, he attended Georgia Southern University under the US Army's Green to Gold program, returning to active duty as a Scout Platoon Leader. Law's Platoon contained a diverse group of Soldiers.

Almost all of his men were veterans of the Iraq war, but none had deployed to Afghanistan. Law admitted, that the deployment "was something we believed we were ready for, but when we got there, we quickly realized that there were some things we were going to have to learn very, very quickly." The platoon had trained at the Joint Readiness Training Center (JRTC) prior to deployment. Law was thankful for the JRTC training in COP defense, particularly since the enemy attempted to overrun his COP several times during his platoon's first months in Badghis.[10]

According to the platoon leader, gaining the trust of the local population and working with the ANA proved a daunting task. Locals observed Red Platoon's activities and reported them to the Taliban. Law's Platoon also initially endured abysmal living conditions. "We had generators that barely worked most days, living in dirt houses where any animal could make its way inside, we had to figure out ways to cool our drinking water, hand washing clothes and gear, [and] living about three to four kilometers away from support," Law lamented. With the construction of COP Metro in October 2010, conditions improved. However, their isolated position, combined with their limited numbers, made the platoon highly vigilant, knowing full well they could be easily ambushed from numerous locations north of COP Metro.[11]

To help defend against enemy attacks, Law built a small observation post (OP) about 500 meters northeast of COP METRO. The new position was called (OP) Liberty. Seven Soldiers of the platoon, rotating with each other every three to four days, manned OP Liberty.[12]

Captain Swaby, the Bulldog Troop Commander, and Law planned for an operation north of COP Metro in the last weeks of March 2011. Law and Swaby spoke via radio and both men used their FBCB2 (Force XXI Battle Command Brigade and Below System) to discuss the enemy situation and a possible course of action. With Bulldog troop spread out, Law pointed out that this was "pretty much how we had to communicate with the Troop Commander, because...he couldn't get out there to us all the time." Both officers wanted to intensify operations north of COP Metro and they intended to take a patrol right up to the enemy's doorstep. Swaby and Law set their sights on the small villages of Kamusari and Joy Gange. Law recalled that they wanted to go there, "basically [into] what [the Taliban] considered their comfort zone." Joy Gange was an important village because it afforded the enemy access to the valley from the north and the population provided support to the Taliban.[13]

Over the course of the next few days, Law's Platoon conducted night reconnaissance missions north of COP Metro. Creek beds provided exceptional cover and concealment for Law's reconnaissance missions. "I used a creek bed, because we could move north and south and not be detected," he recalled. "Nobody could ever see you moving in the creek bed, because the creek bed was maybe seven or eight feet below the ground level. It was completely dried up." Law soon located a vacant compound about 400 meters south of Kamusari Village and determined it made a suitable Observation Post (OP) for the upcoming mission. Petty Officer 1st Class John Pearl, a US Navy videographer, accompanied Law's Platoon on the mission, describing the compound as "ruins." He recalled that the building had no roof and only three rooms. "All the rooms were interconnected by a passageway down the middle. It looked like it was made of mud. I think it had one or two entry points." Law's Platoon named the compound OP Reaper.[14]

Although Law's Soldiers were highly motivated and welcomed the upcoming mission, the platoon leader worried about several issues. First, OP Reaper needed to be fortified, but the platoon was short on sand bags. Law recalled having only a limited number to strengthen the OP. Second, Law was missing his key Non-Commissioned Officers (NCOs). His Platoon Sergeant, Senior Scout, Bravo Team Section Sergeant and two other key sergeants were all on leave. So, I was basically having junior E-5 Sergeants doing the jobs of senior staff sergeants." Yet the manpower shortage did not deter Red Platoon.[15]

On the night of 3 April, Law gave his operations order to the platoon. He named the mission Operation RED SAND, based on their designation as Red Platoon. Law told his platoon that its mission was to observe the area around Kamusari village for enemy activity and conduct a Senior Leader Engagement (SLE) with village leaders in Kamusari. He hoped the meetings promoted greater cooperation between the villagers and the local government. The platoon also intended to conduct patrols throughout the area. Law's intent was to observe activity and "interdict enemy offensive operations." Phase one of the mission consisted of a night move from COP METRO to OP Reaper. Once OP Reaper was cleared, the platoon planned to fortify the outpost. After OP Reaper was established, the plan called for several night reconnaissance missions around Kamusari. At daybreak, Law decided to head straight into Kamusari village to conduct Senior Leader Engagements (SLEs) with the local population.[16]

As part of the move to OP Reaper, Law designated Sergeant Jeff Sheppard as his NCOIC (Non-Commissioned Officer in Charge). Other Red Platoon members included Sergeant Peter Nalesnick, Forward Observer (FO) Specialist Dewayne Sims-Sparks, Medic Specialist Kellen

West, Specialist William Newland, and Private First Class Ben Bradley. Additionally an ANA squad was attached to the force. US Navy Petty Officer 3d Class Ryan Lee and his Explosive Detection Dog Valdo also accompanied Law on the operation. Both Lee and Valdo had worked with the Squadron in the past. Days earlier, Captain Swaby and Bulldog Troop First Sergeant Mike Dempsey introduced United States Air Force Technical Sergeant Kevin P. Wallace and Untied States Navy Petty Officer 1st Class John A. Pearl to Law. Both men were members of a Combat Camera Team. Another section of the platoon, commanded by Staff Sergeant Matthew Fletcher, at OP Liberty, would provide supporting fire if Law made contact with the enemy. [17]

A final attachment rounded out Law's team. Major Lauer, the squadron S3, arrived at COP METRO only hours before Law gave his operations order. Lauer was visiting units, making the rounds across the squadron's area of operations (AO). Lauer recalled talking with Law, "to kind of help him understand why we had directed a mission like this from the squadron level, and how he fit into that larger squadron mission. Because, again, it was a very spread out, dispersed kind of squadron layout, and it was difficult to understand how all these missions impacted each other. For him, it was difficult...to even understand, necessarily, how his operations in the north of the Bela Murghab River Valley were impacting operations in the south." Lauer decided to accompany Red Platoon on the mission, but made it clear that this was Law's operation. "I was merely there as part of battlefield circulation to try to...help explain to them where their role on the larger battlefield was, as well as gather significant understanding for myself, so I could bring it back to the staff, as to what they were facing in that AO."[18]

As part of Law's plan, a Red Platoon Quick Reaction Force (QRF) consisting of two M-ATVs "Mine Resistant Ambush Protected-All Terrain Vehicles" remained at COP METRO under the command of Staff Sergeant Ray Mundo. Law could also rely on Bulldog Troop's QRF located at FOB TODD and commanded by First Sergeant Dempsey if his Platoon encountered serious resistance. The Red Platoon Leader also coordinated indirect fires and Close Air Support (CAS) with the Bulldog Troop Tactical Operations Center (TOC) and the Italian Army located at FOB TODD. In concluding his operations order, Law reiterated the key objectives of Operation RED SAND. A covert movement to the observation post was of paramount importance, as was clearing and establishing OP Reaper. The night area reconnaissance around Kamusari village also remained of upmost significance and required great stealth. Finally, Law accentuated the platoon's paramount goal, "the defeat of all enemy [dismounted] teams in [the] AO." Turning to his men, Law told them, "Hey, it's going to be really cold, and we're going to be getting there at night, we're going to have to dig in. We're going to be up there for at least 24 to 48 hours minimal." The Platoon Leader also advised his men that contact with the Taliban was "expected."[19]

The Mission

At 2300 on 3 April, Law and Red Platoon departed COP METRO on foot. According to Private First Class Ben Bradley, the platoon moved north on Route BRONZE before turning west on a small road toward Kobali village. The patrol moved quickly through Kobali village and then headed north, using the creek bed for cover and concealment. Upon emerging from the creek bed, the patrol worked its way northeast through a field and arrived at OP Reaper at 0001, 4 April.[20]

Upon arriving at OP Reaper, Law's men strengthened the mud and dirt structure. "We fortified the position throughout the night, stood watch, did all those types of typical routine tasks," Combat Camera Team member John Pearl remembered. "I didn't have any night equipment with me, and certainly we were using light and sound discipline," he stated. "So there was really nothing for me to do, except to just go ahead and integrate with the platoon at that point. To be honest with you, this was well outside of my previous experiences. So I was pretty jacked up." Fellow Combat Camera Team member Kevin Wallace helped fill sandbags and placed them in open doorways, of the roofless structure with two to five foot tall walls. "It was just kind of the ruins of a house once upon a time," Wallace pointed out. "There was three distinct doorways to the north that were probably anywhere from two to three feet wide, so we tried to fill those with sandbags the best we could." The men also dug into the floor in an effort to create more space and improve their position.[21]

While the Soldiers fortified the building and stood watch, Law initiated the first of two night patrols into Kamusari village at approximately 0200. "I took a four-man patrol, and we started probing in the village, just identifying routes in and routes out; and just looking for signs of life," Law stated. Valdo and his handler Lee accompanied the patrol. Air Force Technical Sergeant Wallace remembered Valdo sniffing out the village for booby traps, bombs, and IEDs. Law saw few signs of life as his small team crept through the village. Making their way back to OP Reaper, the patrol team managed to catch about an hour of sleep before Law roused his Soldiers for another patrol. At roughly 0400, Law moved his patrol back toward Kamusari village. "*Usually, the locals will come out for prayer around four o'clock, for cooking and things like that,*" Law recalled. Concealed by darkness, the team listened for any signs of activity. The platoon leader remembered trying to gauge "*the activity there, looking to see if there's kids, or if you hear laughing, or if you hear women talking, [any] signs that there's actual normal activities, and not just military age males in that village.*" From the observations, the team concluded that only military-age males were in the village. After a last, quick survey of the village, the patrol headed back to OP Reaper. Major Lauer accompanied this second patrol. Valdo and Lee returned with the team and the bomb dog "*didn't hit on anything the whole time.*" Lauer also pointed out that they were able to walk in and around Kamusari village without any trouble. "*We certainly didn't hear anybody. Very few lights [were] on at all.*" Lauer concluded there was no electrical power inside the village.²²

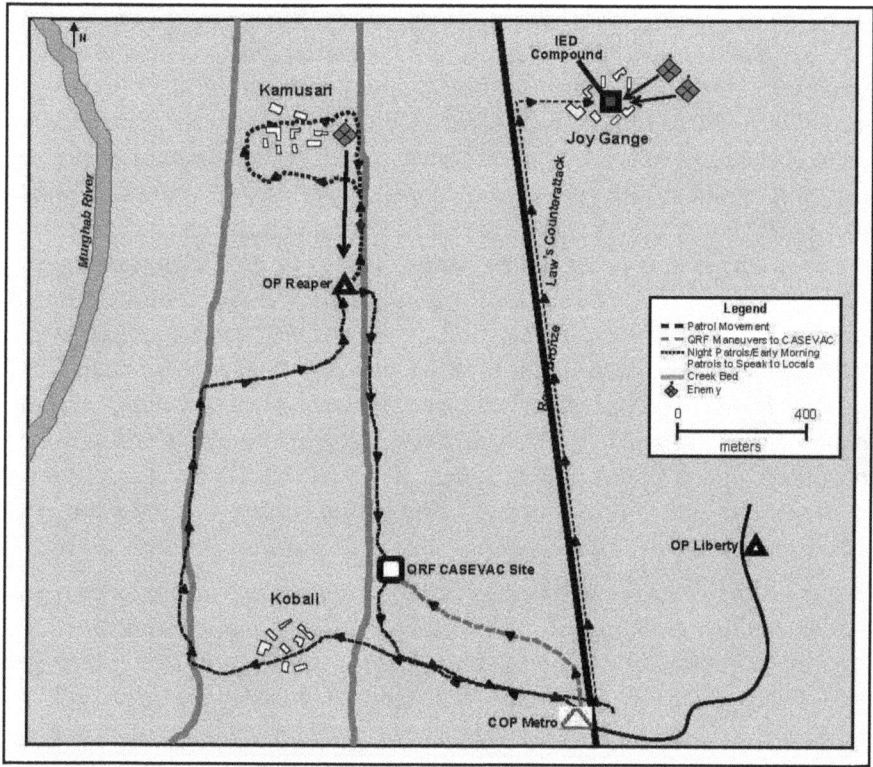

Figure 2. Red Platoon Operations, 3-4 April, 2011.

Upon returning to OP Reaper, Law's Soldiers prepared their positions and watched for signs of the enemy. As the sun came up, the platoon leader saw two males walking out of Kamusari. Wallace reported that they stopped *the men and questioned them. "We tried to assess any information. Is there any Taliban activity going on in the village, or are Taliban present now? We were getting negative responses out of the two people we grabbed. We let them both go and just kind of kept an eye on them, and they headed south across the field down towards where our COP [METRO] was."*[23]

Meeting the Village Elders

After daybreak, Law decided to conduct a SLE with Kamusari elders. He promptly gathered a new patrol team consisting of Major Lauer, Sheppard, Sims-Sparks, Pearl, Wallace, 3 ANA Soldiers and an ANA interpreter. The patrol headed out of OP Reaper north toward Kamusari. "We crept up right on them...we set up a cordon and started doing tactical questioning, talking to some of the older men," Law recollected. Wallace recalled that in the daylight, the village looked like "a waste land."[24]

The SLE did not go well. "It was bad, and very defiant," Law reported. "It goes back to the traditional ways of thinking that they have, that they're not going to change. They're pretty much set on being anti-government... it's something that's really difficult to counter with a group of Americans. They don't have any adult leaders to be...pro-government or...pro-anything different than what they've done for the past thousands of years." Law tried to convince the elders that the Afghan government could help them, but it was to no avail. "The more and more I spoke with them, the more I realized that there was nothing I could tell them that was going to change their mind," Law insisted. Lauer later stated that Law "did a good job of just approaching them and telling them who he was [and] what they were doing. I would say you didn't get the feeling they were happy to see us there, but you certainly didn't get the feeling that they were hardcore Taliban that were out for our destruction. They certainly talked about the Taliban being there. They said, 'oh they all left when you guys came.'" As the conversation continued, more villagers joined the small group.[25]

As Red Platoon members pulled security around Law's conference, a middle-aged Afghan male appeared. He instructed the Americans and ANA that they should leave. Law asked why it was not safe and the Afghan responded, "There's Taliban everywhere." Law replied, "Well, where's the Taliban? Well, they're not here now, but they come all the time. Well, if the Taliban comes all the time, why don't you tell them they're not welcome here?" The Afghan man was growing more and more upset. He emphasized that the Taliban told the villagers that they were the future of Afghanistan and that the Afghan government would lose the fight and the Taliban would be resurgent. Law asked the man if he had been to the district center so he could see what the government had to offer. "When you look around here," Law told the man, "this is what the Taliban can offer."[26]

Figure 3. First Lieutenant Joseph Law, Red Platoon Leader, Bulldog Troop (7th Squadron, 10th Cavalry Regiment) conducting SLE in Kamusari 4 April 2011. Law is on the right.

US Air Force photo/Technical Sergeant Kevin Wallace/RELEASED

At this point, the Afghan encouraged Law to follow him into the village because it was not safe to stay where they were. With Shepherd and Sims-Sparks providing security, safety did not appear to be a problem. The villager, however, claimed that they were being watched. Following him into the center of the village, Law and his team were confronted by four or five other male villagers. Law immediately engaged the oldest Afghan of the group in conversation. "I've been around several Afghans, but I've not seen them act like these guys were," Wallace later stated. "They were angry! They were spitting as they talked, which in their culture is a sign of disrespect, so you rarely ever see them spit in public, but they were spitting when they were talking to Lieutenant Law and our ANA Sergeant, so it was obvious that the conversations weren't going in a positive direction." Wallace concluded that the Afghans were disturbed by the fact that the Americans and the ANA had come into their village and penetrated the northern line of the security bubble. "We were in their backyard, and they weren't happy about it," Wallace emphasized. By this time, Wallace had no doubt that these men were Taliban insurgents.[27]

After about 45 minutes, Law realized the discussions were going nowhere and that the patrol was in a precarious situation. He decided to return to OP Reaper. "I knew as soon as we left, that something was going to go down," Law explained. The platoon leader gave the villagers his contact information and told them that he understood their concerns and would bring them to the Afghan security forces and the Afghan government officials in the district.[28]

Within minutes, the patrol headed south through the village, back toward OP Reaper. As they proceeded through the village, an Afghan villager approached Law's ANA Sergeant and warned him of an IED directly in the patrol's path. The ANA Sergeant then relayed the information to Law. "No we can't go that way, there's an IED over there," he told the platoon leader. Wallace thought this was strange as Lee had just taken Valdo through the area in search of IEDs. However, Wallace stated that Law did not want to take any chances and "brought us around to the other side of the building, so we left in the opposite direction that we came in." As the patrol headed south out of Kumusari, Wallace noticed an ominous sign. As the patrol tramped through the open field back to OP Reaper, Wallace observed about 12 Afghan villagers gathering on top of a two story compound in the village. He watched in horror as other Afghans handed weapons to the men on the roof. Law also saw another portentous sign. While he had not noticed any women or children in the village during the SLE, he now observed at least a dozen running out of the village toward the west. In an instant, the patrol picked up the pace. "We weren't tactically moving... We weren't even scanning for mines, we were pretty much just getting the hell out of there," Wallace recalled.[29]

The Fight at OP Reaper

Law did not know if the Taliban in Kamusari were aware of OP Reaper and he decided to move toward the creek bed and enter the OP from the south. Hastily moving into the OP, Law's men took up defensive positions and waited. In the western room of the OP, Wallace, Pearl, Shepherd and Bradley also took up defensive positions. They were soon joined by Lee and Valdo. Major Lauer, Law, an ANA Sergeant and Sergeant Nalesnick occupied the center room, along with Red Platoon Medic Kellen West. At the same time, FO Sims-Sparks, Newland, the interpreter and the three ANA Soldiers prepared their fighting positions in the eastern room of the OP. "So we got into our respective rooms, and we were talking about basically what had just happened, and anticipating contact," Wallace maintained. As they prepared for a possible attack, West observed Sheppard and Nalesnick walking "the line to police up the guys and ordering them to be on high alert for [a] possible attack." Sims-Sparks then moved into the center room to coordinate with Law to send pre-plotted targets for the mortars at FOB TODD.[30]

Figure 4. Specialist Dewayne Sims-Sparks, 7th Squadron, 10th Cavalry Regiment forward observer, secures a sector of Kamusari Village, 4 April, 2011 in northern Bala Murghab Valley, Badghis Province, Afghanistan.

US Air Force photo/Technical Sergeant Kevin Wallace/RELEASED

Inside the west room, the Soldiers, Airmen and Sailors scanned their sectors for any sign of an attack. As their anxiety increased, Lee told the others in the room, "They're not going to do anything. There's no way.

Nothing's going to happen." As soon as he uttered the last few words, enemy bullets smashed into OP Reaper. "It was just so funny, one tiny line like that, as soon as he said 'Nothing's going to happen' all of a sudden, we have incoming rounds," Pearl declared. At first the OP received only sporadic fire, but soon enemy fire from Kamusari, Joy Gange and the creek bed intensified. "It quickly evolved beyond anything I had ever experienced," Pearl stated. "The magnitude of the rounds, the proximity of the RPGs, [rocket propelled grenades] the accuracy – all those things put me more and more out of my comfort zone. I took a defensive position to make sure that I wasn't struck by any rounds," Pearl remarked. "I continued shooting video, because this was exactly the scenario that you kind of want in my role. So I went ahead, got my camera, and got right to work. As the engagement continued, it became evident we might be in a difficult position, and it may be time to put my camera down, grab my rifle and help the OP defend itself."[31]

In the west room, Wallace watched three enemy rounds slam into the wall inches from Pearl's face. Sergeant Sheppard ordered the cameraman to find a better position and Pearl moved into the center room of the OP. "During breaks in [the] fire we actually laughed and joked about it," Wallace explained. "We were taking extremely heavy and accurate fire from the compound to the north, the canal to the east and the canal to the west." Except for the interpreter, Law's team returned a blistering volley, firing small-arms and grenades. Armed with RPGs, the ANA fired rockets into the enemy positions 400 meters away. Wallace recalled that Specialist Newland and the ANA were "heavily engaged" with the enemy in the eastern creek bed, while the men in the center room were engaging dozens of insurgents in Kamusari. From the western room, Wallace and the others laid down a withering fire into the enemy positions in Kamusari and the eastern creek bed. Wallace also continued to check the southern approach to the OP for enemy fighters.[32]

In the center room, enemy bullets barely missed Nalesnick's head as they slammed into the mud wall. Unfazed by the insurgent fire, Nalesnick laid down suppressive fire on enemy positions in the western creek bed. A torrent of Taliban bullets finally forced him to find better cover. As enemy rounds continued to slice into the OP, Kellen West grabbed his M-14. "I picked up the M-14 and started peeking up over a small groove in the northern wall," he wrote. "I was observing the north calling out enemy locations. I saw enemy dismounts shifting positions and I fired at the moving dismounts as well as the enemies firing in the windows."[33]

> *As the fight grew more intense, Law and Sims-Sparks requested mortar fire on their pre-plotted targets. At the Bulldog Troop TOC, the Italians refused to fire the mission. Law explained "that was something we had a problem with, because the Italian mortars – well, it's different than using the American mortars. Because, as the commander on the ground, if I said...I want you to bring it closer, you know, you can bring it in danger close, [and] the Americans will do it, but the Italians won't do it, because they can actually be tried in a civilian court if something goes bad." As the battle raged conflicting rules of engagement hindered the effectiveness of the coalition Soldiers' fire.*[34]

In the western room of the OP, Sheppard and Bradley engaged enemy fighters in the nearby creek bed while Major Lauer provided cover fire for Nalesnick in the center battle position. From his position on the west side of the OP, Sheppard used his M203 to drop 40mm grenades onto enemy positions in the creek bed. From the east room Newland also put effective M203 fire on the insurgents firing from the creek bed east of the OP. In the midst of the barrage of bullets and incoming RPGs, Law and Sims-Sparks began working up new fire missions for the Bulldog Troop TOC. "At this point," West recalled, "the RPGs started flying over the building originating from the creek bed. Sims threw me the rangefinder and compass and told me to find a target to the west of Kam[u]sari [approximately] 500[meters] out."[35] Incredibly, the Italians still refused to engage the Taliban.

> *Even though we were out of danger close range, I mean I'm looking at the target, I'm trying to hit it, and they refuse to fire on it...Basically, the mortars finally started firing, but they were way off to the west, because they didn't want to [have] any casualties. So, basically... when I'm sitting there telling them where I want it, they refused to take our word...I mean, it was a Taliban squad that we had up in that village, and anybody who was friendly, or innocent, had already left the village.*

It took the Italians approximately 15 minutes to shoot the first fire mission.[36]

Lauer contended that some of the difficulties with the indirect fire stemmed from the dispersed nature of the American and Italian TOCs. He stated that when a fire mission came into the Bulldog Troop TOC, an Italian Soldier would have to run over to the Italian Regimental Headquarters and locate the Regimental Commander. The Italian Soldier "let him know what was going on [and brought] him over to the American [TOC], and then they would...do the fire deconfliction and get the fire mission from the Italians there. The difficult part to it was the accuracy of the Italian mortars, especially when it was rocket-assisted," Lauer recalled. While the Italian rocket-assisted 120mm mortars could range from FOB TODD, Lauer criticized their precision, noting it was "pretty bad." Some of the first rounds to land, exploded uncomfortably close to OP Reaper. "Initially," Wallace reported, "they were hitting right next to us."[37]

In the end, Law was able to "work around" the indirect fire issues. He requested fire for effect on several targets and pointed out that the "mortars [were] not working exactly like we wanted." With the mortars finally in action, Law directed his ANA First Sergeant to fire RPGs at the enemy positions around the OP. Law recalled him "putting them...spot on to where we were taking fire from." The platoon leader also directed his M240 machine gun and M203s on to enemy targets in Kamusari. The combined firepower appeared to be holding the enemy at bay. About this time, Law called for CAS and coordinated with Staff Sergeant Matthew Fletcher and his team at OP Liberty to establish a base of fire with their heavy machine guns on the creek bed to the east of OP Reaper in order to repulse enemy attempts to maneuver through the ravine. Fletcher's Soldiers also engaged enemy targets in Kamusari.[38]

The firefight had been underway for some time when the insurgents began hitting the OP with RPGs launched from the enemy occupied building in Kamusari. "They initially hit the ground in front of the center room," Wallace remembered. "Next they hit the front wall between the center and western room, and then directly hit the wall on the western room." At this point, Lauer, who was helping Law direct fires, told the Platoon Leader, "we probably need to move out of this position." As Law's men redoubled their efforts to suppress the enemy fire, an RPG slammed directly into the west room. The explosion wounded almost everyone in the room. West heard screams and Sheppard and Bradley yelling "Medic! Medic!" West shouted for cover fire and ran into the room. "Upon my initial sweep, all US personnel were still returning fire. Then Sergeant Sheppard began to shout 'get the dog.'" West crawled over to Valdo and Lee and found that the dog was severely injured. "The rest of the US personnel," West noted, "called their wounds out to me...Sheppard shrapnel to the arm... Bradley shrapnel to the leg; Wallace with grazing shrapnel to the neck... Lee claimed no injuries at the time."[39]

With casualties mounting, and a strong recommendation from Major Lauer to leave OP Reaper, Law decided to move back to COP METRO. "We had to get out of there," the platoon leader exclaimed. The men gathered their equipment, prepared to exit the OP, and treated the wounded. West was concerned about bleeding from Sheppard's arm, and quickly made a tourniquet for the wounded Soldier.[40]

Figure 5. Private First Class Ben Bradley (left), and fellow scout Sergeant Jeff Sheppard, engage the enemy from OP Reaper 4 April 2011.
US Air Force photo/Technical Sergeant Kevin Wallace/RELEASED

Law's plan called for the platoon to head for the cover and concealment of the east side creek bed. Once in the creek they moved south, in the direction of COP METRO. With enemy bullets zipping over their heads, Lauer and Nalesnick ran for the creek bed. As they were leaving OP Reaper, a couple of ANA Soldiers fired their RPGs into an enemy occupied building in Kamusari. "Having always been on the receiving end of the RPG, never having been on the outgoing RPG, for me, was fairly interesting," Lauer remarked. "Pretty loud boom as that thing goes out, and then it has a pretty significant morale-boosting effect, to be honest." Wallace was awed by the actions of Lauer and Nalesnick. "They got into contact, when they came down the [creek bed] but they cleared the way for us," Wallace explained. "I was impressed. I mean, this officer kind of running with a scout...to clear the [creek bed]...I haven't seen many things like that in my career!"[41]

As the RPGs fired by the ANA decimated the enemy positions, CAS and an unmanned aerial vehicle (UAV) arrived over Kamusari. An ISAF fighter jet came in low, but instead of dropping bombs, the aircraft popped flares. Enemy fire stopped briefly, but within a minute OP Reaper was once again under a hail of gunfire. Predictably, Wallace and others in Red Platoon did not think the CAS produced the desired effects.[42]

Lauer and Nalesnick jumped into the creek bed and cleared the surrounding area. Next, the S3 radioed Law, informing him that the area was clear. Law's Platoon bolted out of OP Reaper and headed for the creek bed. Eluding sporadic gunfire, the men and Valdo slid down the steep embankment.[43]

With Nalesnick on point, Red Platoon headed south toward COP METRO. As they began to move, Pearl noticed that Valdo could not make the trek on his own. Pearl stated that Valdo was "as much a part of the team as anyone else," and he rushed to help him. "I don't know if it was clear to Petty Officer Lee the extent of the dog's injuries," Pearl remarked. "I think he tried to get the dog to walk through the ditch, and I think the dog actually did that. Quickly it became clear the dog was not going to be able to leave under his own power." As enemy bullets continued to crack overhead, Pearl grasped Valdo and threw him over his shoulders, determined to carry the dog back to COP METRO.[44]

As they hurriedly moved south, Red Platoon remained under constant fire. Lauer worried that the insurgents were maneuvering around them and putting Red Platoon at a "disadvantage." However, Law's Platoon did not realize at the time that they had already accomplished one of their main objectives. As the enemy maneuvered out of Kamusari and Joy Gange, they were spotted by the UAV and CAS. "The CAS was starting to identify people firing at us," Lauer reported. "Not just from where we had initially taken fire, but from the village of Joy Gange out to the east, where we knew there was [a] significant enemy stronghold."[45]

As the platoon continued its trek, Law coordinated with the QRF on standby. After taking the casualties at OP Reaper, the QRF, consisting of two M-ATVs commanded by First Sergeant David Dempsey and Staff Sergeant Ray Mundo, another member of Red Platoon, advanced swiftly out of COP METRO. The M-ATVs headed northwest in the direction of the creek bed. Private First Class Joshua Kukosky explained that Mundo gave the order to "prepare the M-ATVs" as soon as Law called with the casualty report. As they advanced closer to the creek bed, they received enemy fire. In response, they laid down a blistering cover-fire as Law's team emerged from the ravine. The Red Platoon Soldiers at OP Liberty also engaged insurgent targets as the patrol exited the creek bed. "Climbing out of the canal was pretty intense, because you're climbing up and the sides of the canal just break apart as you climb," Wallace recalled. "But, one by one we got the hell out! As I got top side, one of the first things I saw was an RPG bounce off the hood of one of the [M-ATVs] that came to rescue us. It bounced off the hood and flew right over us." Law remembered the weight of his equipment as well as two radios and Mundo jumping out of his M-ATV to help his fellow platoon members. "I got guys bleeding and screaming behind me, and we get up, and we have to crawl out of this creek bed. I look up, and all I see is Sergeant Mundo standing there, and I hear rounds going through the trees, and he's screaming at the guys to start throwing bags up there, to get them out...They had to...physically help us under fire, to get out of the creek bed."[46]

As the men came up out of the ravine, the wounded, including Valdo, were loaded into Mundo's vehicle. West also squeezed in and began caring for the injured. Not all of the Soldiers fit into the M-ATVs, so Law and a portion of his team moved out on foot. "We had to run the whole way," Law stated. "The trucks tried to stay in front of us as much as they could." As they ran, RPGs flew past the M-ATVs and bullets rained down on them. After running about one mile, they finally reached COP METRO. At COP METRO, Sheppard, Lee and Valdo were placed on the MEDEVAC aircraft and taken to FOB TODD. While the rest of the Platoon caught their breath and reflected on the narrow escape from OP Reaper, Captain Tyrek Swaby, the Bulldog Troop Commander radioed Law. "Hey, right now is the best time to go back in there, and really get at them, because we know where they are now."[47]

The Counterattack

Although Law was apprehensive about the new mission, he planned the counterattack immediately with help from Lauer. "It was difficult," Law explained, "I'm missing so many key players...but we've got to put something together right now, because if we're going to get [them], this is the best time to do it." The platoon's reaction to the new order was mixed. Some quipped that the mission was "bullshit," while others were eager to return to the fray. One of Law's men responded "Hell yeah. Let me get my stuff."[48]

As Law, Dempsey and Lauer formulated the plan, the other Red Platoon Soldiers prepared their M-ATVs for the return north. Based on the Bulldog Troop Commander's guidance, the plan called for an assault of Joy Gange. As the planning conference ended, Law turned and yelled, "Hey who's getting in the truck with me." Private First Class Kukosky was the first to respond. Other platoon members followed his lead and piled into the trucks. As the M-ATVs sped north on Route BRONZE, CAS strafed enemy fighters they had identified around Joy Gange. Lauer stated that this "kept the enemy fixed, and...it gave us that breathing space to assemble this force and then push north again towards the village of Joy Gange.'⁴⁹

The two M-ATVs swiftly pushed north. Arriving on the outskirts of Joy Gange, Law, Dempsey and Kukosky dismounted from their trucks and moved toward a compound near the road. "Basically, they dropped us off right there behind the compound," Law explained. "We jumped the wall, all three of us...into this compound not knowing what the hell was in it." As they scaled the wall, the M-ATVs engaged Taliban targets inside Joy Gange with .50 caliber machineguns. Climbing to the top of an outhouse, Law and Dempsey spotted a host of enemy targets in the village. As the trucks laid down blistering gunfire on the targets, Law and Dempsey remained unobserved by the enemy. "They didn't know we were in the compound," Law boasted. "We were basically spotting everything that they were doing, and calling up the trucks." Law recalled that this was one of the first times he had ever witnessed the enemy maneuver against US forces. While the two M-ATVs continued to pound Taliban fighters, Staff Sergeant Mundo arrived on the scene from COP METRO with his M-ATV and joined in the fight. Taking concentrated fire from a building he called the "mechanic's bay," Law called in an airstrike. In no time a jet responded by dropping a bomb on the building and its occupants. As the smoke rose from the building, Law abandoned the compound and moved directly into Joy Gange.⁵⁰

Moving out of the compound, Dempsey radioed his truck, ordering them back to the drop off point. When the M-ATV arrived, the three dismounted Soldiers found that they could not fit into the vehicle because there were already too many people in it. Undeterred, the dismounted Soldiers used the M-ATV as a shield against enemy fire as they approached the western side of Joy Gange. After they had walked about 200 meters, another truck, with open seats, arrived and the Soldiers jumped inside. As all three M-ATVs advanced into the village, some of the Taliban fighters fled north out of Joy Gange.⁵¹

During the firefight, Law observed enemy fire coming from a large compound to the east. While Mundo and a truck commanded by Sergeant James Smith placed suppressive fire on the building, Dempsey's M-ATV careened toward the complex. As the truck jerked to a halt, Dempsey, Law and Lauer dismounted the vehicle and began to clear the compound. By the time they entered, the enemy had already fled. As the Soldiers scanned the complex they found a vast array of IED making material. They also confirmed that the compound was being used for remotely detonating IEDs. "It was wild," Law remarked. "It was like...some crazy professor's lab." The compound would have to be destroyed.⁵²

Figure 6. An insurgent compound explodes after an Air Force B-1 Lancer drops a guided bomb on the facility in northern Bala Murghab Valley, Badghis Province, Afghanistan 4 April, 2011.

US Air Force photo/Technical Sergeant Kevin Wallace/RELEASED

With Lauer present, the team took swift action. Law made clear that, "Major Lauer is the S3...he has a lot of pull with the Squadron, so he can pretty much make the call on the ground that this place needs to be demolished." Lauer lobbed a smoke grenade onto the top of the building as a marker for a circling Air Force B-1 Lancer, and then the three Soldiers quickly mounted Dempsey's M-ATV. As the smoke swirled upward from the roof, all three Red Platoon vehicles sped away from the Joy Gange. As they drove to the east side of Route BRONZE, a 2,000 pound bomb from the B-1 destroyed the IED-making facility. [53]

Although the 2,000 pound bomb leveled the building, it failed to demolish other structures in the compound. When Lauer and Red Platoon returned to Joy Gange to conduct a battle damage assessment (BDA), they discovered another building with IED making material inside and requested that the B-1 reengage. As the team moved back across Route BRONZE, another 2,000 pound bomb fell on the target, completely destroying the structure. Returning to the village, Red Platoon conducted another BDA. This time, however, they encountered sporadic gunfire from north of Joy Gange. Law's Platoon returned fire, and called in CAS, which quickly ended the firefight. Law remembered that, "it went from total chaos [to] probably the quietest I'd ever seen the area." As the Taliban melted away into the hills north of Joy Gange, Red Platoon and its attachments returned to COP METRO.[54]

Aftermath

The tactical impact of Operation RED SAND was truly impressive. Lauer declared that after the fighting in Joy Gange, "the enemy was unwilling to engage us, as well as unwilling to stay in those positions of disadvantage. Just the amount of firepower that we were able to bring to bear during the engagement, it bolstered the confidence of the Afghans, it bolstered the confidence of the population, that we were able to take the fight to the Taliban and win.'[55]

Indeed, Bulldog Troop ultimately cleared all the Taliban from Joy Gange. Shortly after the mission, Red Platoon participated in a village shura and connected the population with the district government. "We even got to the point where we were doing some projects. They were working with the platoon. We were able to get some projects started to help them for working closely with us, and get them some better basic services," Lauer recalled. Clearly, victory in combat had translated into opportunities in governance and reconstruction.[56]

Although Law and his Soldiers fought without their senior NCOs and faced significant challenges with indirect fire, they performed professionally and with valor. Reluctant to sit idly inside the security bubble, the squadron sought opportunities to enlarge its counterinsurgency (COIN) campaign. Despite being shorthanded and saddled with passive coalition partners, the squadron and troop persisted in expanding security and governance within the province. Without doubt, their persistence laid the groundwork for success. The squadron and troop decision to launch Law's counterattack proved decisive. Law's counterattack into Joy Gange seized the initiative from the enemy and led to complete victory.

The ANA Soldiers attached to Law's platoon also performed well and fought bravely in defending OP Reaper. After enemy RPG fire inflicted casualties on Red Platoon, Law's decisive and composed leadership helped restore order. The platoon leader explained that it was:

> *The hardest moment in my life, and as a leader, to deal with that, and hear those Soldiers screaming, and then to hear NCOs screaming, and you don't know if they're OK. You don't know which one's dead. At the same time, you must be able to maintain your composure. And, it was so, so difficult. Try as I might, I can't describe that moment to full effect, to anyone who's never been in that position.*

In the end, all of Law's injured personnel returned to duty. Valdo, the most seriously wounded, was medically retired. [57]

When Law announced his plans for the counterattack into Joy Gange, he displayed tenacious and inspired leadership. While not everyone in the Platoon was enthusiastic about the mission, no one stayed behind. During the counterattack, Red Platoon, First Sergeant Dempsey and Major Lauer exhibited great courage as they fought into the village. During the fight at OP Reaper and the counterattack into Joy Gange, Red Platoon killed 7-12 enemy fighters. Law emphasized that, "The men of Red Platoon took the fight to the enemy and represent the finest of fighting men in America." [58]

Extremely proud of his Soldiers, Law reflected on the fight at OP Reaper and the counterattack into Joy Gange. "The true test of leadership is the willingness of others to follow you into what could possibly be [their] final hours," Law wrote:

> *The pride I keep from the accomplishments of my Soldiers will always be with me. Operation RED SAND broke the backs of the Taliban in north Bala Murghab and paved the way for coalition forces to advance further than we had ever gone. The credit is not due to the general officer or the politician. The credit is due to the Soldiers who [faced] off with the enemy every day. Every victory in Afghanistan is earned on the sweat and blood of the Soldiers.*

Victory on that day was not elusive. [59]

Notes

1. First Lieutenant Joseph C. Law, e-mail to Matt M. Matthews, Combat Studies Institute, Fort Leavenworth, KS, 1 December 2011.

2. Major Jonathan Lauer interview by Matt M. Matthews, Combat Studies Institute, Fort Leavenworth, KS, 5 October 2011, 12; First Lieutenant Joseph C. Law, interview by Matt M. Matthews, Combat Studies Institute, Fort Leavenworth, KS, 26 October 2011, 4.

3. Lauer, interview, 8.

4. Lauer, interview, 11-12.

5. Law, interview, 2; Lauer, interview, 15; Law, e-mail, 14 December 2011.

6. Law, interview, 2; Lauer, interview, 15; Law, e-mail, 14 December 2011.

7. Law, interview, 5.

8. Lauer, interview, 20-22.

9. Lauer, interview, 22-23.

10. Law, interview, 1-2; Law, e-mail, 15 December 2011.

11. Law, e-mail, 15 December 2011.

12. Law, e-mail, 15 December, 3 January, 2011; Lauer, interview, 27-28.

13. Law, interview, 6-8; Lauer, interview, 24.

14. Law, interview, 8-9; Petty Officer 1st Class John Pearl, interview by Matt M. Matthews, Combat Studies Institute, Fort Leavenworth, KS, 27 October 2011, 5.

15. Law, interview, 9-11.

16. Law, interview, 7; First Lieutenant Joseph C. Law, Operations Order for Operation RED SAND, no date, copy author's collection; DA Form 2823, Sworn Statement, Private First Class Ben William Bradley, 4 April 2011, 1.

17. List of Red Platoon members, locations and weapons systems, no date, author's collection; Lauer, interview, 37; Pearl, interview, 2.

18. Lauer, interview, 33-34.

19. List of Red Platoon members, locations and weapons systems, no date, author's collection; First Lieutenant Joseph C. Law, Operations Order for Operation RED SAND, no date, copy author's collection; Law, interview, 9-10.

20. Sworn Statement, Bradley, 1; Law, interview, 11-12.

21. Pearl, interview, 7-8; Technical Sergeant Kevin P. Wallace, interview by Matt M. Matthews, Combat Studies Institute, Fort Leavenworth, KS, 15 August 2011, 6-7.

22. Wallace, interview, 7-8; Law, interview, 12.

23. Wallace, interview, 8-9; Law, 12-13.

24. Sworn Statement, Specialist Kellen West, 4 April 2011, 1; Law, interview, 12-13; Wallace, interview, 9.

25. Law, interview, 13-14; Lauer, interview, 41-43.

26. Wallace, interview, 11-12.

27. Wallace, interview, 12-13.

28. Law, interview, 14; Lauer, interview, 44.

29. Wallace, interview, 13-14; Law, interview, 14.

30. Wallace, interview, 15; DA Form 2823, Sworn Statement, Specialist Kellen Gordon West, 4 April 2011, 1.

31. Pearl, interview, 15-16.

32. Wallace, interview, 16.

33. Sworn Statement, West, 1.

34. Law, interview, 15.

35. Sworn Statement, West, 1.

36. Law, interview, 17-18.

37. Lauer, interview, 46, 48; Wallace, interview, 17.

38. Law, interview, 17-18; DA Form 2823, Sworn Statement, First Lieutenant Joseph Cecil Law, 4 April 2011, 1; Law, e-mail to Matt M. Matthews, 3 January 2001.

39. Wallace, interview, 18; Lauer, interview, 49; Sworn Statement, West, 1.

40. Law, interview, 18; Sworn Statement, West 1-2; Wallace, interview, 23

41. Law, interview, 18; Sworn Statement, West 1-2; Wallace, interview, 23.

42. Lauer, interview, 50-51; Lauer thought the first CAS to arrive was a French Mirage. Lauer, interview, 48; Wallace, interview, 23

43. Lauer, interview, 52; Wallace, interview, 24.

44. Sworn Statement, Bradley, 2; Pearl, interview, 21-22.

45. Lauer, interview, 54.

46. DA Form 2823, Sworn Statement, Private First Class Joshua Travis Kukosky, 4 April 2011, 1; Wallace, interview, 25-26; Law, interview, 22.

47. Sworn Statement, Kukosky, 1; Law, interview, 23-25.

48. Law, interview, 26.

49. Law, interview, 26; Lauer, interview, 57.

50. Sworn Statement, Kukosky, 1; Law, interview, 28-29.

51. *Law, interview, 29-30.*

52. *Law, interview, 31; Lauer, interview, 62-63.*

53. *Lauer, interview, 63.*

54. *Lauer, interview, 63-64; Law, interview, 33.*

55. *Lauer, interview, 64-65.*

56. *Lauer, interview, 64-65.*

57. *Law, interview, 20.*

58. *Lauer, interview, 65; Law, e-mail to Matt M. Matthews, 3 January 2012.*

59. *Law, e-mail to Matt M. Matthews, 3 January 2012.*

Combat Multipliers
Tactical Female Engagement Teams in Paktika Province
by
Michael J. Doidge

Before arriving in Afghanistan in August of 2010, the phrase "You will never leave the Forward Operating Base" may as well have been Staff Sergeant Denise Ferniza's mantra. She lost count of how many times she had heard it. In addition to being a Military Intelligence Systems Maintainer and a Staff Sergeant, Ferniza is a woman. She thought she was going to become what US Soldiers colloquially referred to as a "Fobbit," a reference to J.R.R. Tolkien's "The Hobbit," meaning a Soldier who served overseas but never left the Forward Operating Base (FOB). A month into Ferniza's tour she learned that her unit, the 4th Brigade Combat Team (4th BCT), 101st Airborne Division (Air Assault), was standing up a Tactical Female Engagement Team (TAC-FET). TAC-FETs were designed to assist maneuver units with Afghan women in a number of ways, including the questioning and searching of females during missions that targeted specific insurgents for capture. Comprising ten members at its height and engaging Afghan women in groups of two, those teams would become a 4th BCT asset. Excited and eager, Ferniza volunteered for the team. This was an opportunity to get off the FOB, to get outside the wire, she thought. Within months, the success of the 4th BCT's FET program transformed her mission from a secondary to a primary duty. In fact, by October 2011, she became the team's NCOIC.

In April of 2011 Ferniza and fellow FET member Sergeant Ashley Dixon found themselves on a mission to an isolated qalat, a mud-brick compound in which Afghan families lived. Thirty fear-stricken Afghan women huddled inside. One unruly woman refused to be searched. Dixon yanked up the woman's shirt, revealing what appeared to be a suicide vest underneath. The Afghan women screeched, Ferniza kicked the woman in the chest and she and Dixon bolted out the door. In retrospect, Ferniza flatly stated "I should have shot her. Honestly, I should have shot her. That's what we're trained to do."[1]

She was a long way from the FOB.

Background

Ferniza's journey outside the wire began a year before 4th BCT arrived in Afghanistan when, on 31 May 2010, International Security Assistance Force Headquarters (ISAF-HQ) directed all troop-contributing nations to standardize their engagements with Afghan females. The directive instructed ISAF units to engage Afghanistan's female population in a respectful manner in order to build confidence and support for the

Government of the Islamic Republic of Afghanistan (GIRoA) and ISAF. It stated:

> *Afghan females account for nearly half of the Afghan population and their influence on Afghan society is considerable even when considering local social norms. Therefore, it is important that we conduct engagements with Afghan females to support the battlespace owners' priorities, including, but not limited to, comprehensive understanding of the operating environment, civil-military operations, medical capabilities visits, and educational programs.*[2]

The message was clear: winning in Afghanistan's difficult human and physical terrain required a comprehensive approach toward engaging all of Afghanistan's population.

Afghanistan's cultural customs prevented men from directly interacting with unrelated women. Since most Coalition Soldiers were male, engaging the Afghan female proved challenging. The FET concept inserted female Soldiers into a role that Afghan custom dictated male Soldiers could not perform. Without engaging females, FET member Sergeant Karina Malone warned "[that is] half the society we're not touching;" Coalition forces risked surrendering influence and control over half of Afghanistan's population.[3] *FET enabled the US Army to influence an otherwise overlooked portion of Afghanistan: the Afghan female.*

To gain greater access to the Afghan female, US Army units created ad-hoc FETs to engage the female population through social, cultural, economic, political, and military means. FET tasks generally fell into two categories, tactical (TAC-FET) and operational (OP-FET), although Afghanistan's cultural complexity necessitated that most FETs fluidly shift between the two. The better-known and more common OP-FETs held meetings known as shuras with Afghan females to facilitate political, economic, and social opportunities for Afghan women.[4] *OP-FETs used shuras as a locally sanctioned platform to educate and assist Afghan women and their leaders in family health, community politics, education, and to make them aware of economic opportunities in their area. Whereas OP-FETs buttressed villages against enemy influence by helping Afghan women build and maintain a self-sustaining political, economic, and social support structure, TAC-FETs removed threats to those same villages by assisting maneuver units in combat operations, especially those directed at capturing insurgent leaders. FETs were important during these missions because insurgents commonly hid contraband and intelligence on Afghan women, knowing that US male Soldiers would respect custom and only question and search Afghan males.*[5] *Moreover, Afghan women were not naïve to the goings on in their villages, and they could serve as a vital* resource to Coalition forces.⁶ OP-FETs and TAC-FETs both contributed to the Coalition's counterinsurgency (COIN) approach by contesting the enemy's use of the Afghan female. Denying her use to the enemy aided in building infrastructure, creating security, and establishing effective governance in Afghanistan. With OP-FET embracing local governance and nation building and TAC-FET directly assisting in the elimination of enemy threats, FET as a whole contributed to both the lethal and non-lethal aspects of the Coalition's COIN approach.

4th BCT's TAC-FET often served as an enabler to the brigade's Focused Targeting Force (FTF), an ad hoc unit designed to execute the capture-kill missions focused on known insurgent leaders. Based around the scout platoon from 1st Battalion, 506th Infantry (1-506 IN), the FTF was often augmented by intelligence specialists, explosive ordinance disposal, military working dogs and their handlers, snipers, a mortar platoon, interpreters, and the FET. Though their composition and purpose was not unlike a Quick Reaction Force, rather than react to combat contingencies, the FTF responded to the fluid intelligence environment in Paktika.⁸ When 4th BCT's intelligence specialists became aware that a person of interest or a high value target was in the area, the FTF would act.

When Sergeant Ferniza took on the role of NCOIC of 4th BCT's TAC-FET, the greatest challenge facing the team was the need to increase the proficiency of its members' Soldier skills. The FET needed better Soldier proficiency to be an effective enabler for the FTF. The unit that trained the FTF and FET was comprised of civilian, retired military, and currently serving intelligence, weapons, communications, and medical specialists.⁹ The original FET members' excitement was palpable, "I knew that an opportunity to be attached to an infantry scout platoon was completely unique for a woman... It was exciting."¹⁰ Moreover, "[The group of training specialists] were the pebble that kind of got the boulder rolling because they were the ones who said [the FTF] needed a FET team," Ferniza said.¹¹ The original FET members subsequently underwent three weeks of training in October of 2010. Ferniza said:

> We began with very, very basic Soldiering tasks, weapons systems, optics, lasers, night vision. From that point, we began doing position shooting, barricade shooting, walk and shoots, run and shoots, buddy shooting. We did helicopter landing zone (HLZ), and pick-up landing zone operations as far as how to get on and off helicopters, whether it's a Chinook or a Black Hawk.¹²

For the FET members, the training was eye opening. "The skills were basic infantry skills, just ones that we had never been exposed to...all of this was completely new to me."¹³ Though the FET members agreed the initial training served them well, Ferniza believed that more was needed. "Basic is more than three weeks long!" she said.¹⁴

FET's initial challenges with training were compounded by equipment shortages. "We needed NODs (Night Observation Device). We needed batteries [and] chem lights," Ferniza said.[5] Ferniza's First Sergeant, First Sergeant Brandon Perry, empathized, stating, "The body armor that we give to those guys so they can be lighter and faster...I just -- I physically did not have it...I didn't even have M-4s for all of [the FETs]. Some of them would have...an M-16, or they just had a SAW (Squad Automatic Weapon)...We just didn't have [M-4s]."[16]

Once the FETs became more proficient in Soldier tasks, Ferniza initiated a self-training regimen to expand FET's capabilities. With it, FET also added potential mission roles. Ferniza stated, "The issue that I saw with FET initially...is we had such a pigeonholed role that we weren't worth our weight on these missions. Because if we got to an objective and there were no females, then what?"[17] Ferniza's concerns with the FTF were not unfounded. Though not openly hostile to the FET's presence, at first, the FTF remained wary of the FET's value. To that end, Ferniza insisted FET members conduct combat drills. When Ferniza discovered that the Scouts did not want FET members pulling security, she responded by having FET perform battle and security drills so that they would be prepared for the role if required. "I started doing training on security and battle drills, [to get] us up to par with [the FTF] so we could actually be useful for pulling security," she said.[18] The broadest expansion of FET's mission role came when, drawing from her civilian experience as a nurse's assistant, Ferniza trained her FET members in combat medicine. She believed that a woman's voice could keep a wounded Soldier calm.[19] Where dominant western norms held that men protected caregiving women, Ferniza turned the norm on its head by holding fast to the belief that a female Soldier could protect the male Soldier; in the case of a wounded Soldier, Ferniza argued that a woman's voice on the battlefield helped the male Soldier maintain his calm, protecting him from fear, panic, and exacerbating his wound in the process. When FET did not obtain a medical trainer on the FOB, they used ingenuity by training themselves. Ferniza recalled with pride, "We did a lot of the first training on the actual scouts. We poked them so many times...we're all great at IVs now. We can do those blindfolded."[20] The end result of FET's efforts was greater medical coverage for the entire unit.[21]

Yet their efforts did not stop at combat medical training; Ferniza also strengthened FET's humanitarian aid role by educating her FET members on women's and children's health. Characteristic of her resourcefulness, Ferniza contacted her daughter's pediatrician. "I just talked to her a lot," she said.[22] "I sent her a ton of e-mails...Malnutrition was rampant. We only have so many multivitamins to hand out."[23] She recalled asking the pediatrician 'What's the minimum amount of multivitamins that they can take a week where it's effective?' "[24] But the distribution of vitamins *generated additional tasks, specifically, instruction to illiterate Afghan women on how to properly take vitamins. Again, Ferniza found a solution: she marked the vitamin bottles by prayer schedule. Thrust into a position where their value was not immediately apparent to all in the 4th BCT, the FET carved out a battlefield role and proved their worth as a combat asset.*

4th BCT's FET also trained for specific female engagement tasks, creating a standard operating procedure in the field. Where possible, they would interact with Afghan females in a secure environment, most commonly inside the qalat. There they removed their helmet, eyewear, and gloves to put the Afghan women and children at ease.[25] Many female Soldiers, especially those that engaged Afghans on a regular basis, were issued a head scarf for use in creating a cultural connection during engagements, and FETs were given some measure of autonomy in their use. Ferniza's team rarely wore theirs, preferring instead to use the removal of their helmet, eyewear, and gloves as the primary means of forging a human connection with the Afghans.[26] She believed that revealing the human underneath the Soldier, combined with empathy and sincerity, was the best means to create successful engagements.

Nevertheless, proficiency remained a constant source of frustration throughout the FET's deployment. Continuous personnel turnover challenged FET's capability to keep and maintain highly qualified Soldiers. New FET members received training when Ferniza could provide it, and to 4th BCT's credit, the FET gained a reputation for success. Their success became so great that six months and dozens of FET missions later, 2d Battalion, 506th Infantry (2-506 IN) requested a FET accompany 3d Platoon, Whiskey Company, with their clearance mission during Operation OVERLORD.

Operation OVERLORD

Sharing a border with Pakistan, Paktika Province was extremely poor even by Afghanistan's standards. In the provincial capital of Sharana, electricity came by way of private generators, and only to those Afghans wealthy enough to afford them. In the rural areas, goat herding, firewood gathering, livestock feeding, and mud-clay brick-making dominated local commerce. To the east, the province's harsh terrain and minimal infrastructure permitted travel solely to farmers and their livestock. The Taliban and Haqqani insurgent networks took full advantage of eastern Paktika's rugged terrain to traffic drugs and weapons through areas where US forces rarely ventured. When asked what the conditions were like in east Paktika, Ferniza responded flatly: "Old Testament."[27]

To address these challenges, 4th BCT planned Operation OVERLORD for April 2011 with the purpose of clearing insurgents out of the Naka District in eastern Paktika Province. The bulk of Naka District belonged to 2-506 IN. Naka bordered Sar Hawza District, which was located in

1-506 IN's area of operations. Naka District was small in total area, but possessed a daunting landscape, replete with mountains that towered 12,000 to 13,000 feet in height. Clearing it necessitated the combined efforts of 1-506 IN and 2-506 IN. The combined sweeps were designed to squeeze enemy resistance between the two battalions, and the operation built upon previous US-led efforts to press enemy cells further away from Afghanistan's political and geographic center. In the high peaks of Paktika Province, the Taliban and Haqqani networks assumed that they maintained a permanent sanctuary; the sight of US forces moving through terrain the enemy believed impregnable served as a simple rebuttal. Working with Afghan National Army (ANA) and local Afghan National Police (ANP), the US-led operation planned to remove the insurgent networks, and build ties between the locals and GIRoA.[28]

Naka District was home to a sprawling village settlement of a couple thousand Afghans; clearing it required OVERLORD planners to break the district into sectors and task elements of 1-506 IN and 2-506 IN accordingly. 3d Platoon, Whiskey Company, 2-506 IN drew as their objective a particularly large number of qalats. As noted earlier, 4th BCT leaders knew insurgent males planted incriminating evidence—including weapons, explosives, contraband, and intelligence items—underneath female villagers' clothes. To counter this tactic, 2-506 IN requested a FET as an attachment to its 3d Platoon. Staff Sergeant Ferniza and Sergeant Dixon, both original FET members, were attached to 3d Platoon for the mission.[29]

On 11 April, Staff Sergeant Ferniza and Sergeant Dixon began their ascent to their mission objectives with 3d Platoon, Whiskey Company. After contacting a settlement friendly to 3d Platoon, the unit's movement to their next objective—a nearly unreachable village—slowed to a crawl. At times, the herculean climb took 30 minutes to move 250 meters. Ferniza joked, "Who would build there?"[30] The entire platoon knew this area harbored insurgents. She stated the platoon entered the village "one person at a time...literally pulling yourself up to get up to this place."[31] When Ferniza entered the village, the silence was palpable. The distinct lack of women and children alarmed her, as an empty village was a sure sign of an imminent attack. Ferniza wanted to find the women and children as quickly as possible.

As if in response to her thoughts, she spotted a little girl scurrying across the village. The settlement was small, and she knew the girl could not get far. Ferniza, Dixon, five US Soldiers and some ANA soldiers took off after the girl when they saw her duck into a qalat where 30 Afghan women huddled together. These situations were problematic to FET members. "The issue, and I always preach this to the girls," said Ferniza, "is you never, ever let the women bunch up like that if you can prevent it, *because then you don't know where they live, you don't know who their husbands are, you don't know what they're hiding.*"[32] Determined not to allow FET's duties to degenerate into crowd control, the pair calmed tensions and established a presence to begin searching.[33]

Ferniza and Dixon went to work while the male Soldiers waited outside. Dixon searched the women while Ferniza collected and took pictures of items that might have intelligence value. The FET moved searched women into a separate room, which prevented them from talking and passing materials between each other. Eventually, Dixon came upon a mother desperately cradling her child. She refused to let herself and her baby be searched. "At that point, red flags started just popping," Ferniza said.[34] *When, in spite of the team's insistence, the woman refused to yield, Ferniza threatened, "If you don't do this, the ANA are going to come in here and they're going to search you. We will leave. We'll let the men come in here."*[35] *In the past, the threat convinced recalcitrant Afghan women to comply. This time it was equally effective. The other Afghan women ripped the baby from the mother's hands and pushed her toward Ferniza and Dixon. The mother stubbornly wrapped her arms across her chest and pressed them to her body. Dixon yanked up the woman's shirt and saw what looked like a suicide vest. The Afghan women screeched, Ferniza kicked the woman, and she and Dixon bolted from the building.*[36]

Once outside, Ferniza demanded the ANA enter the qalat to assess the potential suicide threat. Meanwhile, the ANA and US Soldiers gathered all the men in the village for questioning. The village's children milled about idly. Upon entering the room, the ANA discovered the woman was wearing a bandolier of ammunition. Ferniza and Dixon returned to complete their search, ordering all the women to remove foreign objects immediately. Not surprisingly, after the excitement, all of the remaining women were happy to oblige. No other items of interest were found, and the Afghan women were grateful to Ferniza and Dixon for removing the source of potential harm.

Under Ferniza's direct questioning, the recalcitrant mother claimed she found the bandolier in the woods. Ferniza knew she was lying and asked the Afghan woman's husband's whereabouts. The woman responded that he was dead. Having heard this story many times, Ferniza knew how best to approach the situation. After threatening to send the woman to prison for possession of illegal materials, Ferniza went outside to the woman's three-year-old son and gently asked "Where's your papi?" The boy pointed at and went running to his father, who was among the men gathered for questioning.[37] *Ferniza had discovered the owner of the ammunition bandolier without firing a single shot. Moreover, because Afghanistan's conservative culture favored the male, even though the ammunition was found on the wife's body, it was considered the husband's* possession. Third Platoon then destroyed the bandolier and the husband was questioned further.[38]

As 3d Platoon moved to the next part of the village, they intercepted insurgent radio messages that spoke of the unit's movement. Realizing the enemy had identified 3d platoon, the platoon leader halted the movement just as the insurgents attacked with small arms fire. 3d platoon and its attachments returned fire on the enemy positions and, toward the end of the firefight, directed artillery on the enemy's location. Shortly before the rounds hit, enemy fire ceased. Members of the platoon thought the enemy dead; the artillery rounds crashing on the enemy's position assured the US Soldiers that all enemy were killed. The platoon then split up to conduct specific assignments. While some of the men went 300 meters up the hill to perform a battle damage assessment (BDA)—where they found the remnants of several men—Ferniza and Dixon stayed behind and moved inside a qalat to prepare the structure for Whiskey Company's consolidation, bed-down, and eventual extraction from the area. Inside, they were surprised to find a woman and her children. Ferniza and Dixon removed their helmet, eyewear, and gloves.[39]

As noted earlier, FET standard operating procedure was to remove their helmets, and to that 4th BCT's FET added the removal of their gloves and eyewear. One of the most significant acts a FET member could take was to remove her helmet. As all US Soldiers do, FET members risked their lives in a combat environment which recognized no safe havens. They further increased that risk by removing their helmets. Their doing so was to serve the greater mission requirement of creating meaningful engagements with Afghan females. In order to mitigate the risk both to FET members and Afghan women, Ferniza always preached that FET members must perform these engagements in the safest environments possible, those that assure the Afghan female's safety while permitting her whatever creature comforts reasonably available. At the same time, where possible FETs attempted engagements in as safe an environment as possible for the Soldier. Should the engagement produce the desired effect, the rewards justified the FET member's risk. Dr. LisaRe Brooks, the FET training curriculum developer stated: "whether it's taking off the helmet, or putting on a scarf...being mindful of your defensive stance in carrying a weapon, by the Soldier doing that, and then having the reward, as it were, of the Afghan female [lifting] the burqa and [engaging] with you. I think it was a very powerful moment for the Soldiers, because they realize that's the first step."[40]

When Ferniza and Dixon entered the qalat following the firefight, they found the mother and children oblivious to the heavy gunfire that occurred 300 meters from their doorstep. After removing their helmets, Ferniza and Dixon implored the woman to leave, but the woman refused.

"She was in the middle of making her bread," Ferniza remarked, "so I helped her finish that."[41] *To keep the woman calm, Ferniza assured her that the male Soldiers would remain outside. The bread took time to make. With firewood hard to come by in the region, Ferniza understood that this woman would be unwilling to walk away from a working fire. After the woman finished making her bread, she and her children left the qalat. Ferniza's method was the simplest and most efficient means to accomplish 3d Platoon's mission. Since the platoon was already present, and with the rest of Whiskey Company making its way to the bed-down site for consolidation, by taking the time to help the woman make her bread, Ferniza aided in mission success with minimal friction and hostility between US forces and local Afghans.*

Ferniza's act assisted the Soldiers in a tangential way as well. The fireplace was akin to many others in Afghanistan, built underground with pipes running underneath the mud floors to the outside. By keeping the fires going, the floors were still warm when the Soldiers eventually bedded down. The next day, 3d Platoon moved to a helicopter landing zone for movement back to its base. Unfortunately, the aircraft was seven hours late, forcing the unit to remain in a location that was a known insurgent safehaven. Staff Sergeant Ferniza and Sergeant Dixon joined the platoon in securing the landing zone and safely returned with their infantry counterparts. The TAC-FET had made a significant contribution to Operation OVERLORD.

Figure 1. Staff Sergeant Denise Ferniza with Afghan children.
Photo courtesy of Staff Sergeant Denise Ferniza

Bagram: Building on Success

Ferniza's success as a TAC-FET practitioner filtered its way through the U.S. Army's FET community. Following her participation in Operation OVERLORD, she was contacted by the US Army's FET coordinator for Regional Command-East, Lieutenant Colonel Kristine Petermann, who wanted her to teach a training course at Bagram Airfield on TAC-FET operations to about fifty female US Army FET members. Ferniza accepted.[42] She made arrangements to bring with her First Lieutenant Nicole Myers, a fellow FET member and 4th BCT's FET Officer in Charge, to aid and participate in the training.[3]

Ferniza stated that her working relationship with Lieutenant Nicole Myers was symbiotic. The two could not be more different, yet they complimented each other perfectly. Where Ferniza was idealistic and prone to overextending herself, Myers placed Ferniza's concepts into actionable plans. Always professional, detail-oriented, and meticulous, Myers helped legitimize the FET concept, serving as an advocate with both other female Soldiers and senior leaders. If Ferniza was the heart and soul of 4th BCT's FET program, Myers was its energy and face.[44]

The two arrived at Bagram in June 2011 and became primary instructors, delivering seventy-five percent of the teaching during the five day course.[45] Ferniza focused her instruction on the basic soldier skills that she knew from experience had translated into success during Operation OVERLORD and other missions in Paktika Province. Ferniza spoke to the female Soldiers about procedures for conducting the various types of searches, how to participate in flight, vehicle, and convoy operations, and how to set up and properly use their assigned equipment. Later, she moved into FET specific training, where she discussed how to search women and what to expect when encountering Afghan females.[46] The Soldiers praised Myers and Ferniza, and wrote in their after action reports that their soldiering was strengthened as result of the training. Ferniza and Myers felt they had aided FETs from other units to better survive outside the wire.[47] They believed their efforts built a sense of community, as well as esprit de corps within FET. For her part in the training, Myers greatly appreciated the classes in the Pashto language, believing it would add to her tactical competency and ability to contribute to FET.[48] She would have the opportunity to use her language skills soon after returning to FOB Sharana.

Mission to Dila

In late June 2011, First Lieutenant Myers returned from the training course at Bagram to FOB Sharana, where shortly thereafter the FTF leader asked if she and another FET member could serve on a twelve hour mission focused on a person of interest in a small settlement in the Dila District in eastern Paktika Province. Myers was the only FET member available at the time, yet she remembered that Captain Yakena Douglas had previously expressed interest in serving on a FET mission. Captain Douglas served as the Company Commander for 4th BCT Headquarters Company (HHC), and though the demands of command had prevented her from participating in any FET missions, her eagerness to learn and to see firsthand how FETs operated beyond the wire led her to accept and accompany Myers on this mission.[49]

4th BCT's FET program combined a mix of female Soldiers with differing specialties and rank. Each brought their own skillset to the team, but in the interest of keeping everyone safe, the FETs assumed that, when on mission, the person with the most FET experience would lead and give the orders, regardless of rank. Myers summed up the 4th BCT's FET's standard operating procedure succinctly, stating, "We had a 'rank is immaterial' kind of attitude... The FET team leader is the team leader, and that was based on experience and abilities.[50] Therefore, even though Captain Douglas outranked Lieutenant Myers, Myers was the FET team leader for this mission, and it was from her that Douglas would learn. The team members understood that this was their most effective way to operate, as Ferniza stated, "coming home alive was our number one priority, so good experience will always trump rank.'[51]

For the air assault to Dila, the FTF was comprised of a scout platoon, an attached multifunction team of human and signal intelligence specialists, a military working dog team, and the FET, a force of roughly fifty Soldiers in total. Those fifty Soldiers were assigned a single helicopter for transport, but their numbers surpassed its carrying capacity, thus necessitating two lifts to travel from FOB Sharana to FOB Kushmond, and two more lifts to travel from FOB Kushmond to Dila. Arriving at the landing zone after dark, the Soldiers turned on their NODs and began moving. Traveling in single file, the FTF traversed four kilometers to the three qalats located on their mission objective.[52]

Myers stressed to Captain Douglas that long dismounted movements, especially those at night, were about endurance, careful foot placement, and awareness. In April, Myers witnessed a FET member tax her body so greatly on a mission that the Soldier required medical evacuation.[53] Though eastern Paktika was relatively flat, the ground was uneven and the NODs hampered the Soldiers' depth perception. With kit, rifle, and assault pack bringing Douglas' load to 65 lbs, and Myers' heavier assault pack bringing hers to near 90 lbs, Myers did not want a wrong step or too great a strain on her fellow FET member to bring a halt to the mission.[54] However, Myers recalled that the multiple lifts caused the FTF to fall behind schedule; therefore, when the movement to the mission objective began, the FTF leader increased the speed of the movement, thus Myers' talk of endurance for the long slow march gave way to keeping up with the FTF's tempo. Fortunately, Douglas and Myers were well-conditioned for the movement's accelerated pace, and suffered no ill-effects. The FTF arrived at the mission objective at 0200.[55]

At 0230, the FTF moved into the village. The FTF leader began conducting tactical site exploitations (TSE) and questioning at each qalat. The FET was tasked with visiting each qalat where they would question and search the women and children present. Though Myers later observed that the entire village seemed poor even by Afghanistan standards, she noted that the first compound was by far the worst of the three; the ten women and children who lived there looked frail, sickly, and wore threadbare clothes.[56]

Before the FET entered the qalat, Sergeant Scott of the FTF's scout platoon assigned one of his scouts to temporarily assist Captain Douglas in pulling security for Myers while she performed her searches. In addition to the scout, the FET also had a male interpreter with them. Before beginning, Myers placed her weapon with Douglas and turned on her red light lens to assist her search. She removed her helmet, eyewear, and gloves and gently stated in Pashto "aaraam sha" (be calm) to put the women and children at ease.[57] *This was important; the Afghan women and children were terrified.*

Ferniza warned against letting fear take hold within groups of Afghan women and children, who might become unresponsive or bunch up, thus mitigating FET's effectiveness. "Once they start getting en masse like that...FET ends up being crowd-control versus actually doing anything meaningful. I can't hand out medicine...I can't triage. I can't talk to them. It's too hard to deal with that many women," Ferniza stated.[58]

Even in ideal circumstances, the physical requirements of performing searches were enormous. FET members often carried a rucksack weight of between 40 to 70 pounds, while their kit and body armor weighed an additional 40 pounds. To conduct a search, FET members removed their rucksacks, slung their rifles, and squatted low to the ground with each woman and child searched. Complications arose when, as Myers recalled, "You have 50 women lined up to search and your back is killing you and then when they have babies, a lot of the time you're wearing your armor, your full kit, you [often] have your weapon, you're trying to soothe the woman and show them that you're a female, but still remain tactical."[59]

As was commonly the case, in the qalat in Dila, Myers discovered several Afghan women holding their infants at the first compound. In order to search them, she first searched the infant before taking it in her arm. Next she squatted twice, searching the woman first with her free arm before shifting the baby to the other and completing the search.[60] *The village in Dila also fit the standard for Afghan villages in that it held only a handful of males for the Scouts to search and question but dozens of women and children for the FET. The FET's searches were time consuming, and they scolded more than a few Scouts who tried to rush them. Myers found nothing of importance. Following completion of the search, and in preparation for the next mission phase, the FTF leader pulled the scout* from security, leaving Myers, Douglas, and the male interpreter to search and question the women and children at the second compound.[61]

The eight women and twelve children were friendlier and calmer at the second qalat. While Douglas again pulled security, Myers removed her helmet, eyewear, and gloves while again gently stating "aaraam sha" (be calm).[62] Here again Myers found nothing. At the conclusion of the search, and in preparation for the next move, the FTF leader removed the male interpreter.

It was not uncommon for the FTF to order the collection of the Afghan women and children into a single area. Therefore, Myers was not surprised when Sergeant Scott came over to assist her and Douglas in moving the twenty women and children from the second compound into the third, where Myers and Douglas would perform their final FET duty for the mission. Moving the women and children into a centralized location helped the FTF maintain tactical control of the area; it also kept the women and children from disrupting the mission, or worse, endangering their lives or those of the US Soldiers. For their part, the Afghans disliked being moved into the homes of their neighbors, they preferred to be in their own homes.[63]

Sergeant Scott's plan was to lead the women and children to the third qalat in a single file line with Myers and Douglas bringing up the rear. In doing so, Scott would move the line past a structure where elements of the FTF were conducting a TSE. When Sergeant Scott asked in Pashto for the Afghans to follow him, they acted as if they did not hear him. Sergeant Scott repeated the phrase, but again the Afghans did nothing.[64] Finally, Myers spoke, "pa maa pase raaza" (follow me), and immediately the Afghans moved in a single file line behind her.[65] During the movement, a young Afghan teenage girl broke away from the group and began running toward the qalat where elements of the FTF were performing their TSE. Sergeant Scott called out in Pashto for the girl to stop but she did not listen. When he implored, she continued to run. In Pashto, Myers commanded, "Wadarega!" (stop).[66] The girl froze. Myers then stated "Delta raasha," (come here) and the girl moved back toward the group.[67] Finally, Myers implored "pa maa pase raaza" (follow me).[68] The line was restored.

At the third and final compound Myers spoke in Pashto for the women and children from the second compound to sit down and remain calm. She then pulled security while monitoring Douglas as she performed searches on the fifteen remaining Afghan women and children. As with the first and second compounds, the FET found nothing of interest. Following completion of their FET duties, Myers and Douglas assisted the FTF in securing and searching the area.

The time spent on the objective lasted three to four hours. Afterward, the FTF traveled four kilometers to a helicopter landing zone, where it again departed in two lifts. Myers was glad for Captain Douglas' presence, arguing that given the sheer number of women and children on this mission, without Douglas' aid, Myers would have had a lot of trouble managing her duties. She stated that Douglas "handled herself very well, it was her first mission, she was very eager to learn... She used her training and her abilities to the best of her knowledge to help out."[69]

In Afghanistan's culturally conservative climate, 4th BCT's FET admirably demonstrated the US Army's capability to navigate the unfamiliar human terrain, as well as unforeseen challenges common to COIN in Afghanistan. Myers never believed the Afghan girl was in any great danger, yet the girl's actions carried the potential to disrupt the FTF's TSE, and with it, the mission objective. Using her training as FET, her quick thinking, and the advantages afforded to her gender in that circumstance, Myers was able to successfully retake control of a potentially disruptive situation in order to assist the FTF in completing its assigned task. Myers viewed this mission as another milestone in the development of the FET in 4th BCT, stating, "I saw that we were able to use our more advanced FET skills in combination with our soldier skills and help secure and control a situation in a way that the men couldn't have done on their own."[70]

Conclusion

The team's mission successes paid dividends. By the end of their tour, the Scouts used their downtime to teach the FET members some advanced infantry skills, joking that they would make "infantrymen of [them] yet."[71] In another candid moment, Ferniza was standing outside the shower waiting for the male Soldier inside to finish when one of the men she served with saw her waiting and "was confused why [Ferniza] wasn't going in the shower."[72] Epiphany struck the male Soldier, and he laughed as he realized why Ferniza was waiting for the shower to be vacant, sheepishly admitting "forgot you were a girl."[73] He now saw Ferniza as a fellow Soldier. Toward the end of the deployment, Ferniza joked that the FET wished the FTF didn't need the FET so much. However, because the FTF saw their value, "We started going on so many missions. Every single mission we went on, even if it was in the middle of nowhere with no women, we went on it, just in case. Because at that point, we weren't a burden; we were an asset."[74]

However, one challenge 4th BCT's FET never overcame was the issue of competing duty assignments. Ferniza's FET members maintained two lives in Afghanistan, a duty assignment on the FOB and a FET assignment off the FOB. FET member Sergeant Karina Malone stated, "It would've helped immensely in Afghanistan if I didn't have a different full-time [duty] that I also had to do."[75] Ferniza echoed Malone's sentiments, stating "If I got back at seven o'clock in the morning, I'd be up around 8:30, 9:00 [a.m. to perform my duty]."[76] Myers agreed, adding a sharp point to her statement, "It's nice to say yeah, you can take the day off, but we couldn't.

Especially the positions we were in, we couldn't take the day off. We'd go into work, and it was just constant cycle."[77]

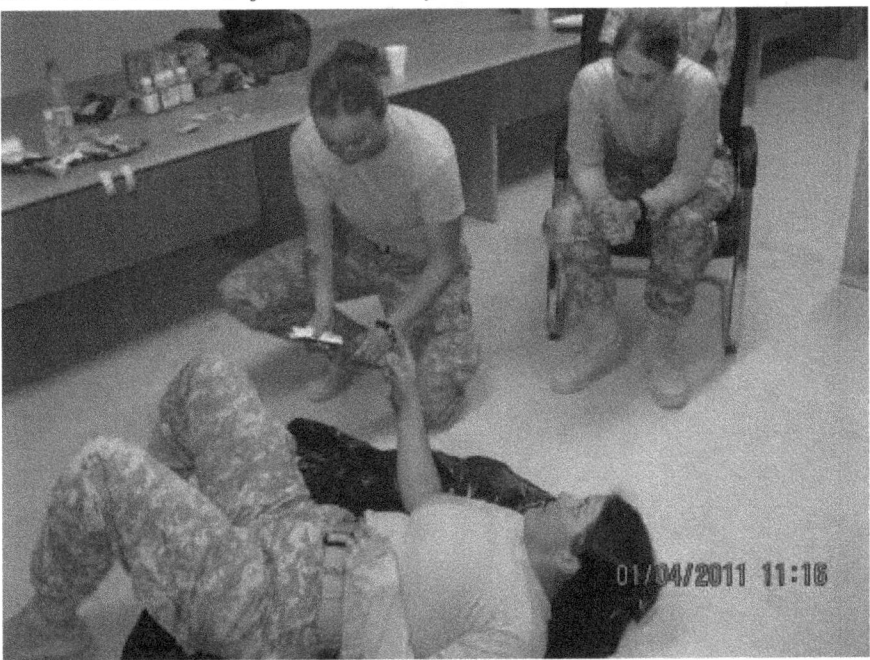

Figure 2. Staff Sergeant Denise Ferniza, front, instructs Sergeant Karina Malone, center, and Private Kasey Anauo in combat medicine.

Photo courtesy of Staff Sergeant Denise Ferniza

Nevertheless, by the end of their year-long deployment, FET's achievements were no small feat. Through 125 missions, 4th BCT's FET aided in the capture of 25 high value individuals, earning in the process three Combat Action Badges, three Bronze Stars, four Army Commendation Medals, and suffering no enemy-related injuries.[78] *Ferniza's FET also led the first TAC-FET conference in Afghanistan, where Sergeant Ferniza and Lieutenant Myers instructed a multi-day class for 50 future Army TAC-FET Soldiers. The FETs built inroads to the women it engaged, diminishing tension between villagers and Coalition forces. She said of the lessened tensions, "I think they felt like our men were less of a threat with women there. Word would get around really fast that women were with the US men. You could just feel it de-escalate."*[79] *One of the chief conceptual architects of the FET program, Dr. LisaRe Brooks, explained that diminishing tensions encapsulated the end result of what FET was designed to achieve. Quoting an Afghan adage, she stated, "Your women are here to help us; your men are here to fight," but she was only half right: Ferniza and her Soldiers could fight.*[80]

4th BCT's FETs were Soldiers first and foremost; and they admirably represented the US Army as cultural ambassadors. Ferniza and Dixon's experiences epitomized this dichotomy; immediately following their firefight with the insurgents, the two FET members enmeshed themselves in Afghan domesticity, helping an Afghan woman to bake her bread. Ferniza stated of those interactions, "If you can just get people talking, you can glean a lot from what they're just conversing about. It doesn't always have to be, 'who's the bad guy?' Just being genuine and nice and helpful...I always brought a picture of my husband and daughter on missions. [I would say,] 'This is my husband, this is my daughter.' "[81] Ferniza removed her helmet to show her gender, but in displaying images of her family to Afghan women, she was emerging from her armor to make a human connection that transcended culture: Ferniza too was a wife and mother. FETs humanized the US-led effort in Paktika to improve quality of life. They engaged in a cultural exchange where the stakes were high, but the potential rewards were higher. The 4th BCT Operations Sergeant Major, Sergeant Major Joseph Singerhouse, stated that FETs' work would foster long-term benefits. "Not only is the mother going to remember... but the kid is going to remember...and that's what the culture over there is. You can give them money all day long, but if they don't trust you they don't care. It's trust. And the [TAC-FET] did that."[82]

Figure 3. Sergeant Ashley Dixon, 4th Brigade FET, on an engagement.
Photo courtesy of Staff Sergeant Denise Ferniza

FET's success had made an impression on the brigade's key leaders. Ferniza recalled being told by her chain of command that her FET had "made a lot out of nothing, [and] done an exceptional job.[83] *The FET's achievements led to a presentation by Lieutenant Myers to Colonel Valery Keaveny, the brigade commander, and he agreed to add a platoon to the brigade whose sole mission was to perform FET missions.*[84] *Located within Charlie Company, 4th BSTB, the new ad-hoc FET platoon was the first of its kind, and were slotted positions for 28 female Soldiers. In addition to language and FET specific cultural awareness and sensitivity training, Ferniza and Myers designed a twelve week training program that will refresh female Soldiers on basic Soldier skills, as well as serve as pre-deployment training for FETs who must be prepared to serve in a combat role if need be.*

The success of 4th BCT's FET was primarily based on several factors: Staff Sergeant Ferniza, Lieutenant Myers, and the entire FET's willingness to always place the mission first, and the support from key members of the chain of command in the 4th BCT. Staff Sergeant Denise Ferniza faced continual challenges with a fierce determination and an ingrained "can-do" spirit. She overcame challenges that would have seriously reduced her program's effectiveness or eliminated it altogether, and the team flourished as result. To marshal her strength, Ferniza drew inspiration from many sources, including noted 19th century leader Mary Harris "Mother" Jones, who married a mother-hen temperament with an innate pugnacity; Staff Sergeant Denise Ferniza embodied her hero. Jones famously opined that she "prayed for the dead but fought like hell for the living." As it turned out, those were the words that became Ferniza's mantra.

Figure 4. The women of 4th BCT who comprised the FET, with Sergeant Major Joseph Singerhouse, Brigade Operations Sergeant Major.
Photo courtesy of Staff Sergeant Denise Ferniza

Notes

1. Staff Sergeant Denise Ferniza, interview by Michael Doidge, Combat Studies Institute, Fort Leavenworth, KS, 2 November 2011, 39.

2. Commander, ISAF, US Forces-A Directive, *Engagement with Afghan Females*, 31 May 2010.

3. Sergeant Karina Malone, interview by Michael Doidge, Combat Studies Institute, Fort Leavenworth, KS, 2 November 2011, 5.

4. Doctor LisaRe Brooks, interview by Michael Doidge, Combat Studies Institute, Fort Leavenworth, KS, 23 November 2011, 10-12.

5. Ferniza, interview, 2 November 2011, 40.

6. Staff Sergeant Denise Ferniza, interview by Michael Doidge, Combat Studies Institute, Fort Leavenworth, KS, 22 August 2012, 15.

7. Malone, interview, 5; First Lieutenant Nicole Myers, interview by Michael Doidge, Combat Studies Institute, Fort Leavenworth, KS, 22 August 2012, 7.

8. Ferniza, interview, 22 August 2012, 2.

9. Ferniza, interview, 22 August 2012, 1-2.

10. Malone, interview, 7.

11. Ferniza, interview, 22 August 2012, 1.

12. Ferniza, interview, 2 November 2011, 4.

13. Malone, interview, 6-7.

14. Ferniza, interview, 2 November 2011, 70.

15. Ferniza, interview, 2 November 2011, 76.

16. First Sergeant Brandon Perry, interview by Michael Doidge, Combat Studies Institute, Fort Leavenworth, KS, 3 November 2011, 13.

17. Ferniza, interview, 2 November 2011, 5.

18. Ferniza, interview, 2 November 2011, 6.

19. Ferniza, interview, 2 November 2011, 5.

20. Ferniza, interview, 2 November 2011, 5.

21. Ferniza, interview, 2 November 2011, 5.

22. Ferniza, interview, 2 November 2011, 58.

23. Ferniza, interview, 2 November 2011, 58.

24. Ferniza, interview, 2 November 2011, 58.

25. Ferniza, interview, 22 August 2012, 16.

26. *Ferniza, interview, 2 November 2011, 61; Ferniza, interview, 22 August 2012, 16.*

27. *Ferniza, interview, 2 November 2011, 59.*

28. *Ferniza, interview, 2 November 2011, 7; Myers, interview, 2 November 2011, 1.*

29. *Ferniza, interview, 2 November 2011, 16; Myers, interview, 2 November 2011 2-3.*

30. *Ferniza, interview, 2 November 2011, 37.*

31. *Ferniza, interview, 2 November 2011, 37.*

32. *Ferniza, interview, 2 November 2011, 38.*

33. *Meg Prior, Documentarian, Outside the Wire, archival footage provided to Michael Doidge, 2012.*

34. *Ferniza, interview, 2 November 2011, 38.*

35. *Ferniza, interview, 2 November 2011, 38.*

36. *Ferniza, interview, 2 November 2011, 38-39.*

37. *Ferniza, interview, 2 November 2011, 40.*

38. *Ferniza, interview, 2 November 2011, 41.*

39. *Ferniza, interview, 2 November 2011, 25-27.*

40. *Brooks, interview, 18.*

41. *Ferniza, interview, 2 November 2011, 28.*

42. *Ferniza, interview, 22 August 2012, 5,10.*

43. *Myers, interview, 22 August 2012, 1.*

44. *Ferniza, interview, 22 August 2012, 10-12.*

45. *Ferniza, interview, 22 August 2012, 4.*

46. *Ferniza, interview, 22 August 2012, 6-7.*

47. *Ferniza, interview, 22 August 2012, 9.*

48. *Myers, interview, 22 August 2012, 1-2.*

49. *Myers, interview, 22 August 2012, 3.*

50. *Myers, interview, 22 August 2012, 4.*

51. *Ferniza, interview, 22 August 2012, 13.*

52. *Myers, interview, 22 August 2012, 5-6.*

53. *Myers, interview, 2 November 2011, 2.*

54. *Myers, interview, 22 August 2012, 8-9.*

55. *Myers, interview, 22 August 2012, 9.*

56. *Myers, interview, 22 August 2012, 12.*

57. *Myers, interview, 22 August 2012, 12.*

58. *Ferniza, interview, 2 November 2011, 38.*

59. *Myers, interview, 3 November 2011, 51.*

60. *Myers, interview, 3 November 2011, 51-52.*

61. *Myers, interview, 22 August 2012, 12-13.*

62. *Myers, interview, 22 August 2012, 14.*

63. *Myers, interview, 22 August 2012, 17.*

64. *Myers, interview, 22 August 2012, 14-15.*

65. *Myers, interview, 22 August 2012, 14-15.*

66. *Myers, interview, 22 August 2012, 14-15.*

67. *Myers, interview, 22 August 2012, 14-15.*

68. *Myers, interview, 22 August 2012, 14-15.*

69. *Myers, interview, 22 August 2012, 4.*

70. *Myers, interview, 22 August 2012, 24.*

71. *Sergeant Karina Malone, e-mail to Michael Doidge, Combat Studies Institute, Fort Leavenworth, KS, 3 December 2011.*

72. *Staff Sergeant Denise Ferniza, e-mail to Michael Doidge, Combat Studies Institute, Fort Leavenworth, KS, 6 December 2011.*

73. *Staff Sergeant Denise Ferniza, e-mail to Michael Doidge, Combat Studies Institute, Fort Leavenworth, KS, 6 December 2011.*

74. *Ferniza, interview, 2 November 2011, 6.*

75. *Malone, interview, 34.*

76. *Ferniza, interview, 2 November 2011, 71.*

77. *Myers, interview, 3 November 2011, 57.*

78. *First Lieutenant Nicole Myers, e-mail to Michael Doidge, Combat Studies Institute, Fort Leavenworth, KS, 31 January 2012.*

79. *Ferniza, interview, 2 November 2011, 67.*

80. *Brooks, interview, 35.*

81. *Ferniza, interview, 2 November 2011, 58.*

82. *Command Sergeant Major Joseph Singerhouse, interview by Michael Doidge, Combat Studies Institute, Fort Leavenworth, KS, 1 November 2011, 27.*

83. *Ferniza, interview, 22 August 2012, 25.*

84. *Ferniza, interview, 22 August 2012, 20-21.*

Securing Dan Patan
A US Infantry Squad's Counterinsurgency Program in an Afghan Village
by
Scott J. Gaitley

After following the trail from Pakistan, the insurgents decided to pay an unexpected visit to the Afghan village of Sharkay where they planned to extort money, weapons, and place vicious demands on the unsuspecting villagers. They had done this many times without challenge. This time, however, the villagers refused the demands. The insurgents responded by kidnapping the son of an elder. The village, for the first time, met the attack with force: a group of trained village policemen immediately confronted the insurgents. After a small firefight ensued, the insurgents broke contact, climbed into a vehicle, and departed the area without the elder's son. The village policemen lacked a vehicle and so could not give chase but they retrieved the elder's son.[1] The villagers in Sharkay had grown tired of playing the role of innocent victims of the insurgency, and had welcomed the idea of a local police force. On this day, that decision had made all of the difference.

From 15 January to 29 December 2011, twelve Soldiers from 1st Squad, 4th Platoon, Alpha Company, 1st Battalion, 16th Infantry (1-16 IN) "Iron Rangers," operated under the mentorship of six elite special operations Soldiers at Combat Outpost (COP) Dandah Patan, in Paktia Province located in eastern Afghanistan (see Figure 2).[2] From here these Soldiers conducted Village Stability Operations (VSO) in conjunction with the Afghan Local Police (ALP) program to establish security within 20 to 25 villages in the region. Historically, Afghan villages defended themselves from harm and potential attacks from outsiders. However, in the face of a virulent insurgency, many Afghan villages in the period between 2001 and 2010 had allowed that tradition to decline. The ALP program encouraged the villagers to revive the practice and win back their independence from the insurgency.

Prior to 1st Squad's arrival, corruption festered within the villages of Dan Patan District and insurgents freely smuggled contraband from Pakistan into the province using the district as a pathway. However, these activities were curtailed once the men of 1st Squad received training from the Special Operations Forces (SOF), gained familiarity with the VSO program, and established close relationships with the neighboring villagers. By the time of their redeployment in late 2011, 1st Squad had successfully trained approximately 350 to 400 local Afghan policemen.[3] The ALP successfully breathed life into a civic tradition, allowing the village populace to stand up for themselves against outside threats, and maintain internal law and order.

Background

The VSO was a bottom-up program that employed United States Special Operation Forces (USSOF) teams to include US Special Forces (USSF) Operational Detachment Alphas (ODAs), US Naval Special Warfare (NSW) Sea Air Land (SEAL) Platoons, and US Marine Special Operations Teams (MSOTs). The VSO program established security, enabled economic development, and promoted governance from the village level up through district and province governments. In addition, VSO strategically focused on Afghan communities resisting the Taliban and other insurgent groups through grass-roots initiatives (local efforts to strengthen communities), especially in areas with limited Afghan National Security Forces (ANSF) and NATO-led International Security Assistance Force (ISAF) presence.[4] As noted earlier, VSO was grounded in a tradition of rural Afghan villages providing basic self-defense and community security, with the support of the Government of the Islamic Republic of Afghanistan (GIRoA). These were not militias, a term often used in Afghanistan to refer to large forces under the command of individual warlords. Instead, VSO relied heavily on small, defensive, village-level policing entities under the supervision of local shuras (decision-making councils comprised of village elders).[5]

The VSO initiative developed into a four-phase process: shape, hold, build, and transition.[6] The shape phase began with an assessment of the village and surrounding area and ended with the establishment of a US Special Operations VSO site within the village. This phase "may be the most critical," claimed Lieutenant Colonel Olivier Wache, Advisory and Assistance Team VSO officer-in-charge, and was characterized by building rapport, trust, and relationships with the Afghan villagers, a three-month long process.[7] During the hold phase, VSO personnel focused on protecting the rural population and laying the foundation for follow-on development and self-governance efforts. The build phase linked villages to district and provincial governments through institutional arrangements, such as district and provincial shuras, and carefully designed and managed development projects using Commanders Emergency Response Program (CERP) funds and other resources. CERP projects were designed to promote civil infrastructure in Afghanistan by providing money to tactical forces, enabling them to meet emergency civilian needs, such as irrigation projects, road refurbishing, and school construction.[8] Finally, the transition phase expanded village stability to other areas throughout a district, while transitioning responsibility for security, development, and governance to the Afghan government.[9]

Many factors were considered before determining a VSO location: force protection, logistics, the population's assent, population density, tribal compositions, security and economic effects and the likelihood of being able to expand influence beyond the initial site.[10] Often, village elders requested police or military forces to increase security. However, tribal and ethnic dynamics played a big part in deciding where SOF chose to embed. The program had to be sure that VSO sites would not aggravate existing prejudices against a certain tribe or ethnic group. Tribal differences in the various locales played a crucial role in regulating the distribution of power, money, and resources.[11] Lieutenant Colonel Wache stated, "It's always easier when the population was from one ethnicity, because there are less struggles."[12] Afghan villagers throughout the Dan Patan District were of the Pashtun ethnic group and often accepted the VSO program with enthusiasm. Still, many villages remained under the influence of the insurgency.

The Role of Afghan Local Police (ALP) in Village Stability Operations

After considering the recommendations of General David H. Petraeus, Commander International Security Assistance Force (COMISAF), Afghanistan President Hamid Karzai approved the establishment of the ALP program in mid-August 2010 to improve Afghan security in select locations.[13] The ALP facilitated counterinsurgency (COIN) operations by further expanding and extending security through village stability operations in remote areas. Operating at the village level, ALP provided public protection in communities that lacked ANSF.[14] The ALP had no arresting authority nor did they earn as much pay as the ANP. However, the program found success. By 31 March 2011, approximately 4,518 ALP members had completed training with another 282 Afghans in the process of becoming operational members (see Figure 1).[15] By 17 June 2011, the Ministry of Interior (MoI) reported 41 validated districts with 6,400 community-selected ALP members. Continued expansion and success of the ALP program faced several challenges. The Taliban and other insurgent groups countered ALP growth and success with a campaign of targeted assassinations, nighttime threat letters, intimidation, and kidnappings. In several areas, intra-tribal and inter-tribal tensions prevented ALP *expansion. The ALP was just one part of a comprehensive VSO program and was not the only component of VSO success; on occasion, the ALP operated independently from the VSO program.*

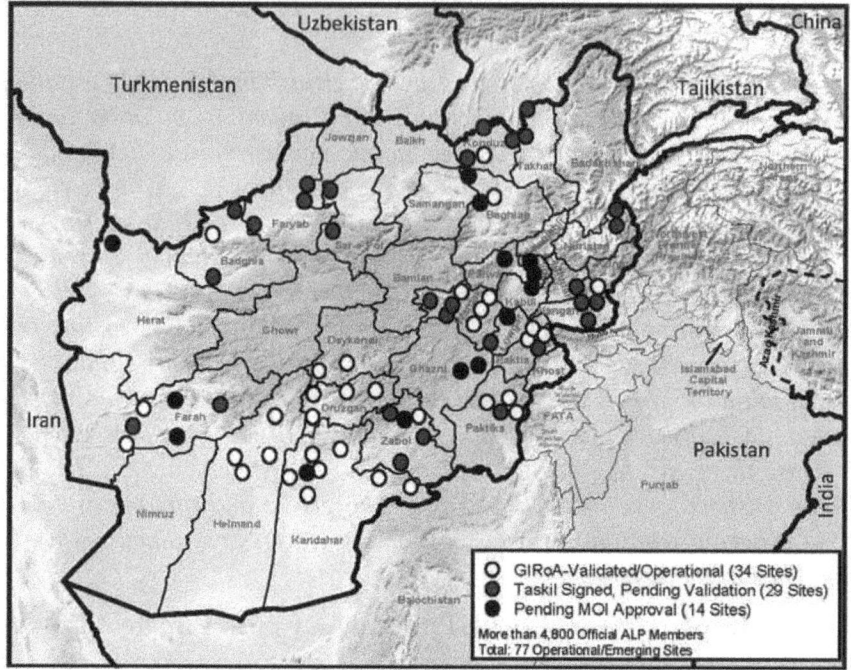

Figure 1. Afghan Local Police sites (as of 31 March 2011).[16]

Those ALP personnel who had completed their required training organized village watch teams, served as an early warning and initial village defense elements against insurgent activity, and provided a pool of qualified personnel to join the ANA or ANP. On average, it took almost six months before an ALP unit was operational. However, the district of Dan Patan was an exception to this policy; their ALP program was successfully operational in a matter of weeks. Longevity of a particular ALP unit was dependent on the situation at each location, the effectiveness of the element, their interaction with other Afghan forces, and the prevention of developing militias.[17]

The rising concern about militias and warlord-type entities encouraged ALP sites to develop in a deliberate manner, ensuring sufficient time for assessment of local area dynamics, structured training, arrangement of an oversight system, and implementation of remote support procedures in coordination with USSOF and ISAF tactical units responsibility for a particular area. Once the number of ALP sites expanded at a pace congruent with Afghan government capacity for oversight and USSOF and/or ANA SOF capacity for partnering, some sites with greater potential transitioned from SOF to GIRoA control and oversight.[18]

By late 2010, the ALP program had reached a turning point. Additional forces were needed to continue the expansion of ALP sites in Afghanistan, and SOF capacities were at their limit. Conventional forces were considered as the necessary work force required to attain the ALP objectives. Recognizing this, in December 2010, General Petraeus placed a conventional US Army infantry battalion, the 1-16 IN from Fort Riley, Kansas, under the operational control of special operation forces in Afghanistan; its mission was the expansion of the VSO and ALP programs.

Task Force *Iron Ranger*

Between 2006 and 2008, the Iron Rangers conducted COIN and advisor training to Foreign Service personnel and advisor teams preparing for deployments to Afghanistan and Iraq. In May 2009, the battalion discontinued its COIN training mission and formed into a combined arms (heavy brigade combat team) unit. Many enlisted instructors (E-6 and above) assumed new duties as squad leaders and platoon sergeants.[19] Scheduled for a deployment to Iraq in September 2010, the battalion conducted training on basic battle drills, convoy tactics, counter improvised explosive device (IED) techniques, combat life saving courses, and weapons qualification.[20] Twenty-two days prior to their expected departure date, the orders to Iraq were canceled. Shortly thereafter, the battalion was informed of their forthcoming VSO and ALP mission in Afghanistan. The Iron Rangers living up to their unit's motto *Semper Paratus* (Always Ready) were anxious for the new challenge.

In preparation for VSO/ALP in Afghanistan, the Soldiers received basic pre-deployment and combat skills training for their new role, which included language instruction. With Arabic no longer required, they learned one of several Afghan languages. Captain Joseph Frego, a platoon leader in Delta Company, explained, "The language program used depended on what site you were going to, and introduced the Soldiers to Dari, Farsi, or Pashtu."[21] The Iron Rangers received reference pamphlets for language and basic communication with the Afghans along with computer-based training on Afghan culture. However, nothing prepared them for the total immersion into Afghan society. The most fortunate Soldiers received an in-brief with SOF personnel after arriving in-country and prior to departing to various locations throughout Afghanistan. SOF team members discussed their personal experiences with the Afghan villagers, culture, community relations, and explained some of the most prevalent obstacles that the Iron Rangers might experience during their tenure.²²

Approximately 689 Soldiers from the 1-16 IN, under the command of Lieutenant Colonel James J. Smith, deployed to Afghanistan on 15 January 2011.²³ Their area of operations extended throughout many of Afghanistan's 34 provinces. The battalion distributed Soldiers to 52 different sites. One of the battalion's units, Alpha Company, sent four platoons (174 men) to 17 isolated locations in four different provinces, where they operated independently. The company had 138 Soldiers assigned, however, Alpha Company's First Sergeant Danny R. Conley, requested 36 additional men (mostly mechanics, medics, and cooks) to enhance the VSO mission at several sites that lacked the necessary support facilities and personnel. The largest sized unit in one location was a 44-man platoon, whereas the smallest was a three-man fire-team.²⁴ These elements often found themselves isolated and without assistance from the battalion.

Alpha Company's 4th Platoon was primarily comprised of "tankers," crewmembers who operated M1A2 Abrams tanks. This unnerved First Sergeant Conley, who stated that "Tankers, rarely are seen on patrols...doing movements to contacts, kicking down [doors] and clearing buildings."²⁵ Conley knew that in order for these men to survive in Afghanistan that they needed some "trigger pullers" or infantrymen. Therefore, "I put my best infantry squad with them and it paid off significantly," he said.²⁶ That unit, designated 1st Squad, consisted of 10 assigned infantrymen and two attached Soldiers.

The 1st Squad benefitted from the presence of smart and experienced leaders who had once instructed advisor teams in COIN operations. Staff Sergeant Shawn Goggins, Squad Leader; Staff Sergeant Mathew Carson (who assumed the duties of squad leader on 1 July 2011, when Goggins returned to the States); and Sergeant Kenneth Eunice, A-Team Leader were tactically sound and proficient in everything they did. In fact, Goggins was the epitome of an Army infantry leader and his Soldiers followed his example. "Goggins was the most stellar soldier in the brigade," said Conley.²⁷ When Conley had first met Goggins nearly six years earlier, Goggins was a private but still stood out among the new enlisted Soldiers in the battalion. Since that first introduction, Goggins had earned the title of honor graduate for the Warrior Leader Course and regularly achieved perfect scores on his Army physical fitness tests and earned a Bachelor's Degree in Criminal Justice. In September 2006, he deployed to Iraq as part of Charlie Company, 1-16 IN. As a squad leader, Goggins was responsible for his Soldiers daily activities and performance and ultimately, became an *adviser, trainer, role model, and supervisor to his Soldiers. His mentoring capabilities and leadership qualities ensured that 1st Squad was ready for the challenging aspects of its ALP duties. "We were looking forward to it...it was a different mission than what we were used to...we knew there was going to be a multitude of challenges...but overall everybody was pretty excited for the specialized mission," stated Goggins.*[28]

Alpha Company arrived in Afghanistan in mid-January 2011. After spending nearly 30-days at Bagram Airfield receiving training and instructions from SF members on VSO/ALP operations, three squads from 4th Platoon convoyed for two days to their final destinations. Sergeant Daniel Taylor, 1st Squad's Forward Observer, explained that, "Each squad drove a total of three mine-resistant ambush protected vehicles that were assigned to them for the duration of their deployment."[29] *Sergeant Goggins and his squad arrived at Dandah Patan and joined 6 ODA members from 20th Special Forces Group (SFG) (US Army National Guard), 2 US Civil Affair Team (CAT) personnel, and 12 Afghan National Army Special Forces (ANASF) that collectively conducted VSO duties.*[30] *In March the 20th SFG was replaced by the 3rd SFG. Dandah Patan was a rural agrarian community adjacent to the Pakistan border (see Figure 2). Dandah and* Patan were two separate villages divided by the Daryā-ye Chamkanī *Stream; however, the Afghans considered them one collective location.*

The ODA in Dandah Patan had concluded the shape phase within the VSO initiative, and now more Soldiers were required for implementing the next two phases. 4th Platoon would assist the ODA and separate into three squads and a headquarters element. Each squad would then operate in separate districts within Paktia Province. The platoon's three squads focused on protecting the rural population and laying the foundation for follow-on development, as part of the hold phase. 1st Squad operated from Combat Outpost (COP) Dandah Patan. 3rd Squad and the headquarters element were located 10 to 12 kilometers away at Chamkani district center. And 2nd Squad operated from COP Herrera, roughly 20 to 25 kilometers northwest of Dandah Patan in extremely mountainous terrain.[31]

The Village of Dandah Patan

In mid-2008, due to the lack of Coalition Forces in the district and the easily traversable terrain, the insurgency began using the Dandah Patan area for their supply lines (rat lines) originating in the third largest arms bazaar – Teri Mangel Post – inside Pakistan. From this location, approximately 20 kilometers to the north of Dandah Patan, the insurgents smuggled weapons and other vital supplies into Afghanistan.[32] *An Afghan villager named Khalid working as an electrician for the US Military at Firebase Chamkani, first mentioned the insurgent movement in this remote area to USSOF team members.*

Shortly thereafter, SF personnel dispatched an ODA to talk with the Dandah Patan villagers to ascertain the feasibility of establishing a VSO within the region.[33] *The insurgent smuggling operations continued unabated until the fall of 2010, when an ODA from the 20th SFG began conducting ALP operations in the region. These SF Soldiers instructed the ALP training course and visited Dandah Patan daily. Afghan workers constructed COP Dandah Patan less than one kilometer west of the Pakistani border. This strategically-placed COP hindered insurgent operations and forced them to move their rat lines further south into treacherous mountainous terrain, making it more difficult for them to transport supplies. However, more Soldiers were needed to assist the ODA with establishing close relations with the Afghan villagers and training ALP. This was the mission of Staff Sergeant Goggins' squad.*

Upon their arrival at COP Dandah Patan 1st Squad found only sparse accommodations. The Soldiers began constructing latrines, a dining facility, a storage area for dry food, and sleeping quarters for themselves and their newly appointed teammates. It took several months to establish the base, but the Soldiers began conducting joint patrols immediately and meetings with village elders – known as key leader engagements (KLE) – followed shortly thereafter. Goggins and his men integrated with SF personnel, they conducted joint patrols, shared meals, and bedded down in the same quarters. The ODA "provided guidance when we needed it, but were very good about not micro-managing us while we completed daily tasks," said Sergeant Kenneth Eunice.[34] *The 1st Squad and ODA Soldiers worked harmoniously. Other squads from 1-16 IN were not so fortunate, enduring caustic relations with their SF counterparts.*

Hold Phase Operations

Sergeant Goggins explained that as part of the hold phase, their initial mission of supporting the ODA included providing physical security during village KLEs, assisting in the training of ALP personnel, and personally visiting neighboring villages. Goggins knew that the Soldiers would be working closely with the Afghans; he just did not expect it to happen "every single day."[35] *But the Iron Rangers attempted to overcome any obstacles in order to achieve their mission as they averaged two to three weekly village visits. During the course of its deployment, 1st Squad made regular visits to approximately 20 to 25 villages in four different districts (Dan Patan, Chamkani, Sabari, and Akmhad Kheyl) and in two adjoining provinces (Paktia and Khost).*[36]

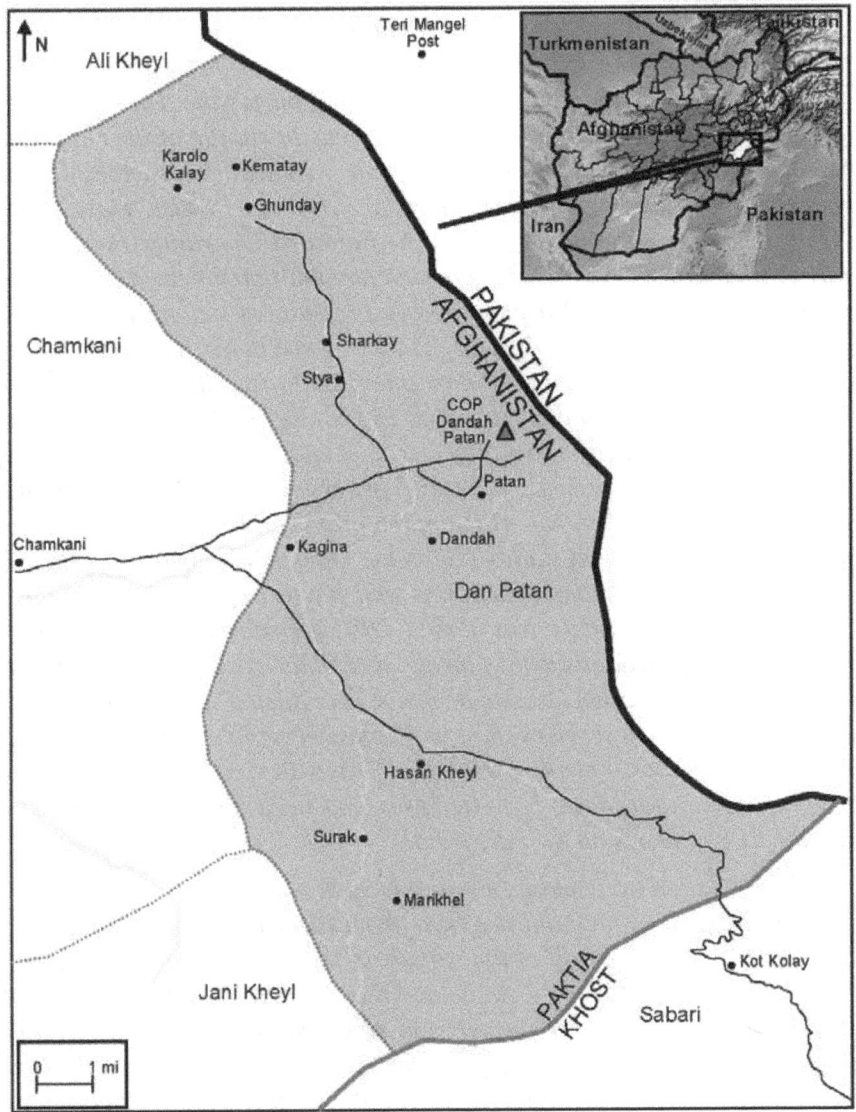

Figure 2. Dan Patan district geographical reference map.

Sergeant Goggins' management style, skills, and techniques enabled effective communication and organization, while his demeanor encouraged positive relationships between his Soldiers and the members of ODA. The ODA mentored the Soldiers of 1st Squad and instructed them on firing mortars and other special operation skills unfamiliar to the average

133

infantryman. 1st Squad eventually formed a mortar team that effectively engaged targets in the district. As 1st Squad gained proficiency in its VSO duties, responsibility was irreversibly transferred from ODA personnel to members of the squad. Goggins wrote the program of instruction for the ALP training course and maintained military order within the COP. Sergeant Eunice assumed the duties of pay agent for the ALP graduates. Sergeant John Friedman, B-Team Leader, was in charge of the rifle range and basic marksmanship. Sergeant Taylor was lead instructor for ALP trainees. Specialist Gene Larue, Assistant A-Team Leader, traveled by CH-46 Chinook helicopter routinely to Forward Operating Base (FOB) Gardez where he picked up weapons and ammunition for the ALP training course and implemented accountability procedures among the Afghans for these items. Specialist Antoine Waters, a mechanic, ensured that all 32 vehicles at COP Dantah Patan operated safely for daily missions, and used his civilian culinary training to provide the COP with hot food. Specialist Zachary Guynn, a Rifleman, coordinated the advanced training for the ANASF who assisted in the ALP program, but required their own remedial training when an ALP course was not in session. Specialist Michael Shepard, Squad Radio Telephone Operator, learned the intricate art of radio satellite communications and how to operate and repair all types of communication devices at the COP. He ensured connectivity with Alpha Company headquarters, patrols, and other coalition assets. Private First Class John Miller, a combat medic, conducted more direct patient care and emergency services than he witnessed on television growing up in the United States. Private First Class Travis Barrett, Squad Designated Marksman, monitored the base defenses and used his weapons skills to educate ALP trainees on the rifle range.[37]

    The 1st Squad executed its mission in such a professional manner that if First Sergeant Conley did not hear from them for some time, he was not concerned. "Out of all of the squads in the company, I didn't have to worry about them."[38] Conley concluded that if ODA departed the district, 1st Squad could take over the mission singlehandedly. The ODA Team Sergeant informed Conley that if not for Goggins, 1st Squad would have been nowhere near as effective. As the deployment progressed, 1st Squad conducted patrols as an organic infantry squad without any assistance from the ODA. These patrols included trips to Ghunday, Karoto Kalay, and Kematay (see Figure 2). Conley believed that if the ODA went into an area to implement the VSO shape and hold that his conventional forces could build and prepare for thetransition, providing that the Afghans facilitated this process as well as they would in the villages of Stya, Kagina, and

Dandah Patan (see Figure 2). The ALP from these three villages conducted security patrols as far north as Sharkay and voluntarily projected Afghan security throughout the district.

Relations between the Soldiers and the Afghans differed depending on a number of factors including personality conflicts between Afghans and Americans, insurgent influences in the specific region, and elder opinions of the ALP program. Goggins never felt his Soldiers were in any imminent danger while working with the Afghans.[39] He felt that the Pashtunwali, the Pashtun code of behavior that ensured protection for guests, provided for their safety.[40] Sergeant Friedman, a team leader in 1st Squad, was actually surprised at the high amount of support the local population gave the Soldiers, and how tranquil and considerate most of them were.[41]

Further south of Dandah Patan, the VSO program faced challenges in the village of Hasan Kheyl, Marikhel, and Surak (see Figure 2), where the insurgency had significant influence and contributed to the failed attempt at ALP operations there. The code of Pashtunwali was not as apparent to the American Soldiers as in other locations. In an attempt to encourage positive relations with the inhabitants of Dan Patan District and establish the build phase of VSO, members of 1st Squad and ODA set-up a medical civil assistance program (MEDCAP) and visited the district center and various villages where they provided medical service to many Afghans. Working with a civil affairs physician and a SF trained medic provided Private First Class Miller with the rare opportunity to provide direct care including advanced care of wounds for scores of patients. Often, the villagers walked great distances to the COP, carrying their loved ones for medical treatment. Miller recalled that a significant number of the Afghan children suffered from cancer and other long-term ailments.[42] Other humanitarian efforts such as CERP projects were used to win over the villagers and open their minds to the possibilities of the VSO program.

The use of CERP funds for development projects was a contested part of VSO. Due to villager demands and tribal conflicts, the SF had to learn how to harness the effectiveness of money to foster community relations rather than encouraging corruption. In the village of Ghunday (see Figure 2), CERP funds contributed to the population's quality of life, such as the construction of a bridge that enabled local children to cross a river, shortening their walk to school and the renovation of the district center, a project that encouraged economic prosperity after a major insurgent attack.[43] Throughout Afghanistan, the VSO utilized CERP projects – humanitarian aid, medical and veterinarian assistance, improved farming technique classes, hydro-electric generator installation, road building and improvements, and basic village repairs – to benefit the population.[44] However, there are instances when the use of CERP did not guarantee a village's support in the ALP program or strengthen security in the region as proven by the persistent influence of the insurgency in the village of Hasan Kheyl, where the ALP never gained a foothold.

ALP Trainees and Graduates

The district governors, sub-governors, and village elders were essential in recruiting their own ALP candidates, a critical component in the successful build phase.[45] The applicants that met specific requirements for enrollment needed to be between the ages of 18 and 45, live in the village they intended to secure, and be nominated and validated by a local and district Shura member. They had to have a valid tazkera (Afghan identification document), pass a health screening, and drug test, pass a district chief of police screening and interview process, and complete three-weeks of training before being validated by MoI.[46] Finally, they had to undergo an extensive two-week vetting process conducted by the ODA. At Dandah Patan, the ODA communications sergeant handled all the vetting and background checks. This process included fingerprinting and photographing each potential candidate before they could join the training program. Shortly after 1st Squad gained familiarity with the vetting process, Specialist Shepard assisted with the identification cards, interviews, and ALP in-processing.

To build rapport between the US Soldiers and their ALP counterparts, the ODA and 1st Squad made certain accommodations in their program. Since the vast majority of the trainees walked to their ALP courses, class times varied throughout each course in accordance with the distance traveled by its attendees. A typical class scheduled for those in the Dandah Patan area began at 0800 or 0900 hours. Allowing for an hour for lunch and mid-day prayer, the class might conclude for the day at 1500 or 1600 hours. Providing allotments for prayer time enhanced cultural relations between US Soldiers and Afghans. During routine remedial instruction upon graduation, the ALP remained overnight for two or three days of training. Prior to the commencement of each initial ALP training course, the district governors attended, demonstrating their support for the program.[47]

During their training, the ALP was instructed on the laws of armed conflict and various military subjects that included marksmanship, radio communications, first-aid, IED detection, vehicle checkpoint security, search and detection, and drug interdiction. Initially, ALP marksmanship *training was conducted using the Samopal Vzor SA Vz-58 assault rifle, but the ALP trainees complained about this weapon. Specialist Larue explained, "It kicked too hard and was far too difficult for the Afghans to zero in."⁴⁸ He then swapped out the SA Vz-58s and obtained 125 AK-47 assault rifles. Approximately 24 to 28 hours was spent on the rifle range over a three to four day period during the initial ALP course.⁴⁹ While on the rifle range, Larue taught the prone, kneeling, and standing rifle firing positions to the trainees. Sergeant Friedman had set-up three-inch targets at 25 meters for the Afghans to shoot, all with mixed results. Training not only enhanced the skills of the ALP personnel, but also boosted their confidence to the point that if they came under attack, they could defend themselves.*

Trainees were provided with every opportunity to graduate from the ALP course. However, some of the selected villagers failed to take the course seriously, did not grasp the mental or technical challenges, or invariably made mistakes. Many trainees lacked the ability to read and write, but Afghan interpreters ensured that each student understood the classroom principles preceding the field training. Prior to the graduation ceremony, a panel of ANASF, ALP Commanders, ODA, and 1st Squad instructors reviewed each trainee and discussed their progression and limitations. Ultimately, this panel decided on those who passed, those that needed to retake the course, and those that failed.⁵⁰

Upon successful completion of the three-week training program, the district governors and sub-governors held a graduation ceremony for the ALP trainees. Each graduate then visited Sergeant Larue and received an AK-47 assault rifle, six 30-round magazines, uniform vest (weapons rack), medical kit, sleeping bag, an all-purpose utility tool, a personal hydration system, a set of desert camouflaged rain gear, and thermal underwear. Upon receipt of their gear, the ALP graduates reported to the ALP commander for their assigned duties.⁵¹

ALP graduates assisted SOF and 1st Squad in expanding "white space," those areas inhospitable to the insurgents and thus hospitable to the establishment and solidification of legitimate local governance.⁵² For example, "white space" included the areas surrounding villages – a strategic road or hilltop that ALP and US Soldiers patrolled on a routine bases – denying these areas to the insurgency. The village elders and ALP created the defense plan for their communities, Guynn recalled.⁵³ ALP personnel conducted outer security for neighboring communities, directed vehicle checkpoints, organized route security, and assisted with improvised explosive device (IED) recovery. 1st Squad had carefully trained ALP for the dangerous IED mission because the threat in the district was so serious. Sergeant Friedman noted, "We would build makeshift IEDs out of whatever we could find. We'd dig them on the inside of the compound or training area for them."[54] *If an IED was discovered, "They established a 360-degree perimeter and cordoned off 100-meters distance away from the suspected device, then finally called it in via cell phone to the COP via interpreters," elaborated Specialist Larue.*[55] *The ODA engineer sergeant was then dispatched to the designated location for the destruction of the IED.*

Every two months, between March and December, Sergeant Eunice flew to FOB Salerno in neighboring Khost Province and obtained the Paktia Province CERP funded ALP payroll. Each ALP member was paid 9,000 Afghani ($203), while the commanders were paid 12,500 Afghani ($284).[56] *ALP members returned to the COP and presented their weapons to Specialist Larue for accountability (serial numbers and names matched to each weapon) and then they received pay from Eunice. Salary disbursements were based on the proof that the ALP member had their weapon and the ALP Commander attended to verify that a weapon was missing. "No weapon, no pay" was the policy. First time offenders received a warning and were denied pay until a weapon was available. The second time they were dismissed from the ALP program. Denial of pay and other disciplinary measures were handled by the ALP commanders. Sergeant First Class Travis Hutt, Platoon Sergeant for 3rd Platoon, Charlie Company, explained that in the village of Kushkadir, Uruzgan Province, "Weapons were inevitably sold to insurgents and sometimes the ALP commanders had to round-up the weaponry whenever possible."*[57] *Although this was not a common occurrence in Dandah Patan, the leaders of the ALP sought to ensure that no ALP member in the village even considered the sale of his weapon.*

Periodically, Soldiers from 1st Squad held three-day refresher training sessions for the ALP graduates. Initially, this was done in conjunction with payday, with the Afghans receiving their salary on the first day and the training continuing for two additional days. However, "We realized that they're not going to come in on the second and third days. So we separated it. They'd come in three days, train, and then later on they'd get paid that month," explained Eunice.[58] *Towards the end of the deployment, refresher training decreased due to the increased number of missions to outlying villages.*

The ALP in the Dan Patan District was more successful than programs in other districts. For example, in the Maruf District of Kandahar Province,

Sergeant Andrew Blascyzk, a Team Leader for 1st Squad, 1st Platoon, Delta Company, had difficulties convincing Afghan villagers to join the ALP. He recalled what the locals told him, "We don't need to protect ourselves, it's your job, that's what you're here to do, so you figure it out, you protect us."[59] Often, the ALP participants threatened to quit if things were not in their favor. This was especially true when pay was late. There were times when funding was not readily available, and the trainees had to wait an extra month for their salaries, but they were eventually compensated.[60] Sergeant Goggins felt that the ALP trainees in Dandah Patan and its neighboring villages of Stya, Kagina, and Sharkay believed in what they were doing. It was apparent to 1st Squad which ALP members were motivated by pay and those who desired a better way of life.

Transitioning

Fifteen village elders from the most active villages in the district typically participated in the program as ALP commanders. As part of the transitioning phase, the village assumed control over the training program at Dandah Patan. In the fall of 2011, "Elders came in to take over the training of new recruits and did so very well," claimed Sergeant Eunice.[61] The elders and commanders facilitated all types of training except on the rifle range, which remained under the direction of the ODA and 1st Squad. The elders also conducted physical training and various types of tactical training, allowing the Afghans a chance to train one another.

In late fall, 1st Squad traveled 15 to 20 km south into Khost Province, where they conducted KLEs with villagers and attempted reestablish relations that had been allowed to languish. Sergeant Eunice was pleasantly surprised at the warm and friendly reception in the village of Kot Kalay (see Figure 2).[62] This extensive eight hour trip was only made possible with the arrival of additional Alpha Company Soldiers at COP Dandah Patan, who then assumed control of 1st Squad's duties in their absence. 3d Squad, 3d Platoon, relocated from FOB Lilly after several 107mm insurgent rockets struck the base, destroying a 5,000 gallon fuel bladder and nearly the entire FOB in the fire that ensued. 3d Squad remained at COP Dandah Patan until December. While Kot Kalay in fact had ALP personnel, its numbers were insufficient for any meaningful security operations.

Still, visits to distant villages like Kot Kalay had value. Eunice explained the benefits of engaging the Afghan populace with "boots on the ground," instead of projecting military power in armored vehicles. He recalled villagers telling him, "How can you trust someone who tells you to do this, but they hide in their vehicles."[63] With this in mind, the Soldiers parked their vehicles off in the distance and walked into the *villages they visited. Members of the 1st Squad reiterated the importance of interacting with the villagers at the lowest level. The amount of personal integration with the villagers surprised many of the Soldiers, and Sergeant Larue stated, "It was a great experience for me and I would love to do it again."* [64] *The Afghans appreciated how the VSO Soldiers talked with them attempting to understand their requirements for a healthy, stable, and peaceful livelihood. As Afghans and US Soldiers routinely conducted "boots on the ground" patrols that deterred insurgents from returning to once-contested areas, the ALP instituted local security, enabled economic development, and promoted governance. Immediate engagement with the newly "liberated" villagers and the establishment of "white space" demonstrated the benefits of rejecting insurgent influence and cooperating with the GIRoA.*

Sergeant Friedman recalled from his Dandah Patan experience, "I've witnessed some ALP members come forward and show great potential in retaining information that we have taught them, and also reassert themselves in front of their fellow ALP members." [65] *Friedman hoped that the successful training of ALP members ensured the continuation of a successful program, one that made a real difference in the security and safety of their respected villages. When working with the Afghans, Soldiers often wondered if what they did mattered in the grand scheme of things, and Specialist Waters was no different.*

Specialist Waters, in his spare time, trained the ANASF on proper vehicle preventative maintenance and basic repairs. One of his proudest accomplishments was instructing them – without an interpreter – on changing a battery in a Humvee. After completing his class, each Afghan could complete the task. The ANASF Team Sergeant realized the advantages of American vehicle maintenance procedures and began following their example. Whenever his men completed a mission they refueled the vehicles, removed personal articles and weapons, and conducted preventative maintenance on each vehicle. "What I taught them, actually worked," proudly exclaimed Waters. [66]

One negative outcome during Sergeant Goggins tenure was the planned transfer of US military equipment including ammunition, magazines, field gear, sleeping bags, vests, and four Polaris Ranger all-terrain vehicles, to the district police who were to distribute it to the ALP. [67] *Apparently, this transaction never occurred, because ALP members from the northern areas visited Dandah Patan requesting the equipment selected for transfer. Later, the vehicles were found near the district center. Because of this incidents like this, when the locals needed anything, they would go to the*

COP and ask 1st Squad for assistance, bypassing the district government representatives. This showed that while the VSO/ALP program made great strides in fostering Afghan villagers' capacity to protect their communities, there remained a lack of confidence and a disconnect between the villagers and their respective GIRoA representatives.

Conclusion

At the village level, the ALP program within VSO worked effectively at Dandah Patan, Stya, and Sharkay, but failed because of the insurgent influence at other Dan Patan district villages, such as Hasan Kheyl, Marikhel, and Sultak. The VSO methodology of shape, hold, build, and transition worked as more Soldiers trained, supported, and empowered the tribes to do the right thing and protect themselves. However, the level of success could vary widely. The program introduced ALP to 20 to 25 villages, but only three had effective and functioning programs implemented by the collective efforts of the ODA and 1st Squad from COP Dandah Patan. The effect of these three successful programs was magnified as ALP members from Dandah Patan, Stya, and Kagina patrolled throughout many of the neighboring villages. Each VSO had its own peculiarities and was only as successful as the investment of the Afghans. Frequently, whenever the Soldiers suggested a change to the ALP, it was well received and emphatically carried out. Members of 1st Squad periodically conducted random patrols to certain villages to see which ones were conducting their ALP duties properly, and as soon as the Soldiers entered the villages, they were offered Chai tea and the ALP members automatically joined the US Soldiers in donning their vests, grabbing their weapons, and providing security.

Building relationships of rapport and trust with the Afghans was crucial for a successful shape phase and the final transformation to the transition phase within the VSO/ALP program. Based on his personal experience and relationships with the Afghans, Sergeant Goggins believed that "We could have gone on a mission and walked in villages north of our area with nobody ever armed. We felt completely safe." [68] *First Sergeant Conley added, "I probably wouldn't have been afraid to put on my PTs on and run through the village on PT, because that's how quiet it was. If something was going on, ALP would let the teams know."* [69] *Sergeant Eunice, added that the Squad's relationships with the Afghans, "Grew over time and became very strong."* [70] *In many other districts where the Iron Rangers trained ALP members, the Afghans refused to do anything under their own initiative without an American presence for motivation and guidance. "It was like pulling teeth to get them to help defend themselves," explained Sergeant*

Hutt [71] *This same frustration reverberated throughout the battalion. Still, 1st Squad had enjoyed more than a little success in the villages of Dandah Patan, Stya, and Kagina whose populace saw it as their duty to protect themselves from insurgents. These were the Afghans who would take the initiative to do what was needed without direction from the Soldiers.*

The key to VSO and the successful implementation of ALP members in Dandah Pata was the face-to-face relationships based upon mutual respect. A positive relationship between the population and their security forces was one of the most effective counterinsurgency efforts. With a mobilized populace, the villages of Dandah Patan, Stya, and Kagina were able to stand up for themselves to project physical security in outlying communities against outside threats, while maintaining internal law and order.

Notes

1. Staff Sergeant Sean K. Goggins, e-mail to Scott J. Gaitley, Combat Studies Institute, Fort Leavenworth, KS, 18 January 2012, 1.

2. CPT Jacob K. Moulin. E-Mail to author, 16 November 2011, 1:28 p.m. Subject: RE: VSO, Afghanistan. Combat studies Institute, Fort Leavenworth, KS.

3. First Sergeant Danny R. Conley, interview by Scott J. Gaitley, Combat Studies Institute, Fort Leavenworth, KS, 26 January 2012, 11; Carson, interview; Sergeant Zackery K. Guynn, interview by Scott J. Gaitley, Combat Studies Institute, Fort Leavenworth, KS, 25 January 2012, 2.

4. Lieutenant Colonel Olivier Wache, interview by Lieutenant Colonel Brian White, ISAF, Kabul, Afghanistan, 24 June 2011; 2-3; Report to Congress. "Report on Progress Toward Security and Stability in Afghanistan." November 2010, 67.

5. Report to Congress. "Report on Progress Toward Security and Stability in Afghanistan." November 2010, 67; Sean D. Naylor. "Program has Afghans as First Line of Defense." Army Times, 20 July 2010.

6. Captain Rory Hanlin. "One Team's Approach to Village Stability Operations."Small Wars Journal, 4 September 2011, 1.

7. Wache, interview, 5.

8. Lieutenant Colonel Brian Petit. "The Fight for the Village: Southern Afghanistan, 2010." Military Review, May-June 2011, 29; Captain Neiman C. Young. "4th and Long: The Role of Civil Affairs in VSO." Special Warfare, 24, no. 3 (July-August-September 2011): 18.

9. Colonel Ty Connett and Colonel Bob Cassidy. "Village Stability Opera.. tions: More than Village Defense." Special Warfare, 24, no. 3 (July-August-September 2011): 24-27; Captain Neiman C. Young. "4th and Long: The Role of Civil Affairs in VSO." Special Warfare, 24, no. 3 (July-August-September 2011): 19-20.

10. Chief Warrant Officer 3 Stephen N. Rust. "The Nuts and Bolts of Village Stability Operations."Special Warfare, 24, no. 3 (July-August-September 2011): 30.

11. Rory Hanlin. "One Team's Approach to Village Stability Operations," 6; Wiebke Lamer and Kathleen Hughes. "Village Defense: Understanding the Afghan Local Police (ALP)." Civil Military Fusion Center, Afghanistan Monthly Report, July 2011, 1; Lieutenant Colonel Brian Petit. "The Fight for the Village: Southern Afghanistan, 2010." Military Review, May-June 2011, 29.

12. Wache, interview,16.

13. Sean D. Naylor. "Karzai Says He Will Back Locally Based Forces." Military Times, 14 July 2010, 1-2; Sean D. Naylor. "Program has Afghans as First Line of Defense." Army Times, 20 July 2010, 1-5.

14. Wiebke Lamer and Kathleen Hughes. "Village Defense: Understanding the Afghan Local Police (ALP)," 1.

15. Wiebke Lamer and Kathleen Hughes. "Village Defense: Understanding the Afghan Local Police (ALP)," 2.

16. US Department of Defense. "Report of Progress Toward Security and Stability in Afghanistan and United States Plan for Sustaining the Afghanistan National Security Forces, April 2011, 62.

17. Wache, interview, 6-7.

18. Report to Congress. "Report on ProgressToward Security and Stability in Afghanistan." November 2010, 69.

19. Staff Sergeant Mathew J. Carson, interview by Scott J. Gaitley, Combat Studies Institute, Fort Leavenworth, KS, 25 January 2012, 7.

20. Sergeant Andrew E. Blasczyk, interview by Scott J. Gaitley, Combat Studies Institute, Fort Leavenworth, KS, 20 October 2011, 3.

21. Captain Joseph C Frego, interview by Scott J. Gaitley, Combat Studies Institute, Fort Leavenworth, KS, 19 October 2011, 3.

22. Staff Sergeant Robert N. Conley, interview by Scott J. Gaitley, Combat Studies Institute, Fort Leavenworth, KS, 19 October 2011, 3.

23. Moulin, E-Mail, 16 November 2011.

24. First Sergeant Danny R. Conley, interview by Scott J. Gaitley, Combat Studies Institute, Fort Leavenworth, KS, 26 January 2012.

25. Conley, interview, 9.

26. Conley, interview, 7.

27. Conley, interview, 10.

28. Goggins, interview, 3.

29. Sergeant Daniel Taylor, interview by Scott J. Gaitley, Combat Studies Institute, Fort Leavenworth, KS, 25 January 2012.

30. Goggins, interview, 4.

31. National Geospatial Intelligence Agency. *Afghanistan Country Atlas Series Volume 3: Ghazni, Kabul, Khost, Laghman, Logar, Nangarhar, Paktika, Paktiya 1:50,000*. National Geospatial Intelligence Agency, 2009, M1779; Staff Sergeant Sean K. Goggins, interview by Scott J. Gaitley, Combat Studies Institute, Fort Leavenworth, KS, 19 October 2011, 5.

32. Goggins, interview, 4 & 10.

33. Goggins, interview, 10.

34. Sergeant Kenneth Eunice, e-mail interview by Scott J. Gaitley, Combat Studies Institute, Fort Leavenworth, KS, 11 January 2012, 3.

35. Goggins, interview, 5.

36. Carson, interview, 5.

37. Conley, interview, 9; Sergeant Kenneth Eunice, interview by Scott J. Gaitley, Combat Studies Institute, Fort Leavenworth, KS, 25 January 2012; Sergeant John Friedman, interview by Scott J. Gaitley, Combat Studies Institute, Fort Leavenworth, KS, 25 January 2012; Sergeant Gene D. Larue, interview by Scott J. Gaitley, Combat Studies Institute, Fort Leavenworth, KS, 25 January 2012; Sergeant Daniel Taylor, interview by Scott J. Gaitley, Combat Studies Institute, Fort Leavenworth, KS, 25 January 2012; Specialist Antoine Waters, interview by Scott J. Gaitley, Combat Studies Institute, Fort Leavenworth, KS, 26 January 2012; Private First Class John Miller, interview by Scott J. Gaitley, Combat Studies Institute, Fort Leavenworth, KS, 26 January 2012; Guynn, interview.

38. Conley, interview, 10.

39. Goggins, interview, 5.

40. Seth G. Jones. "It Takes the Villages: Bringing Change From Below in Afghanistan." Foreign Affairs, May/June 2010, 3.

41. Sergeant John Friedman, e-mail interview by Scott J. Gaitley, Combat Studies Institute, Fort Leavenworth, KS, 11 January 2012, 1.

42. Private First Class John Miller interview by Scott J. Gaitley, Combat Studies Institute, Fort Leavenworth, KS, 26 January 2012.

43. Specialist Antoine Waters, e-mail interview by Scott J. Gaitley, Combat Studies Institute, Fort Leavenworth, KS, 11 January 2012, 1.

44. Captain Scott J. Weeman, e-mail interview by Scott J. Gaitley, Combat Studies Institute, Fort Leavenworth, KS, 28 December 2011, 5.

45. Carson, interview, 5.

46. HQ, CJSOTF-A. "Village Stability Operations and Afghan Local Police: Bottom-up Counterinsurgency." 1 April 2011, 38.

47. Carson, interview; Sergeant Zackery K. Guynn, interview by Scott J. Gaitley, Combat Studies Institute, Fort Leavenworth, KS, 25 January 2012.

48. Sergeant Gene D. Larue, interview by Scott J. Gaitley, Combat Studies Institute, Fort Leavenworth, KS, 25 January 2012, 4.

49. Friedman, interview, 3.

50. Specialist Travis Barrett, interview by Scott J. Gaitley, Combat Studies Institute, Fort Leavenworth, KS, 26 January 2012, 7.

51. Larue, interview, 4.

52. HQ, CJSOTF-A. "Village Stability Operations and Afghan Local Police: Bottom-up Counterinsurgency." 1 April 2011, 52.

53. Guynn, interview.

54. Friedman, interview, 6.

55. Larue, interview, 8.

56. Eunice, interview.

57. Sergeant First Class Travis D. Hutt, interview by Scott J. Gaitley, Combat Studies Institute, Fort Leavenworth, KS, 19 October 2011, 9.

58. Eunice, interview, 4.

59. Sergeant Andrew B. Blasczyk, interview by Scott J. Gaitley, Combat Studies Institute, Fort Leavenworth, KS, 20 October 2011, 7.

60. Goggins, interview, 5.

61. Eunice, e-mail interview, 3.

62. Eunice, interview, 1.

63. Eunice, interview, 7.

64. Larue, interview, 12.

65. Friedman, e-mail interview, 2.

66. Waters, interview, 10.

67. Goggins, interview, 7 & 11.

68. Goggins, interview, 12.

69. Conley, interview, 11.

70. Eunice, e-mail interview, 2.

71. Hutt, interview, 5.

Glossary

ABP	*Afghan Border Police*
ABVs	*Assault Breacher Vehicles*
ANA	*Afghan National Army*
ANP	*Afghan National Police*
ANSF	*Afghan National Security Forces*
AO	*Area of Operations*
APOB	*Anti-Personnel Obstacle Breaching System*
ARF	*Aerial Reaction Force*
ASIP	*Advanced System Improvement Program radio*
ASR	*Alternate Supply Route*
ATPIAL	*Advanced Target Pointer Illuminator Aiming Light*
AUP	*Afghanistan Uniformed Police*
AWG	*Asymmetric Warfare Group*
BCT	*Brigade Combat Team*
BDA	*Battle Damage Assessment*
BSTB	*Brigade Special Troops Battalion*
C2	*Command and Control*
CAT	*Civil Affairs Team*
CAV	*Cavalry*
CCA	*Close Combat Attack*
CCP	*Casualty Collection Point*
CERP	*Commander's Emergency Response Program*
CFPDM	*Currahee Focused Police District Mentoring (Program)*
CFSOCC	*Combined Forces Special Operations Component Command*
CJSOTF	*Combined Joint Special Operations Task Force*
COIN	*Counterinsurgency*
COP	*Combat Outpost*
CP	*Command Post*
CROWS	*Common Remotely Operated Weapon Station*
EOD	*Explosive Ordnance Disposal*
FA	*Field Artillery*

FET	*Female Engagement Team*
FO	*Forward Observer*
FOB	*Forward Operating Base*
FTF	*Focused Targeting Force*
GBUs	*Guided Bomb Units*
GIRoA	*Government of the Islamic Republic of Afghanistan*
G-MLRS	*Guided-Multiple Launch Rocket System*
HHC	*Headquarters Company*
HLZ	*Helicopter Landing Zone*
HVT	*High Value Targets*
IED	*Improvised Explosive Device*
IJC	*International Joint Command - ISAF Joint Command*
IN	*Infantry*
IOTV	*Improved Outer Tactical Vest*
ISAF	*International Security Assistance Force*
ISR	*Intelligence, Surveillance, and Reconnaissance*
JDAMS	*Joint Direct Attack Munitions System*
JLENS	*Joint Land Attack Cruise Missile Defense Elevated Netted Sensor System*
JRTC	*Joint Readiness Training Center*
JTAC	*Joint Terminal Attack Controller*
KIA	*Killed In Action*
L&O	*Liaison and Observer*
LMTV	*Light Medium Tactical Vehicle*
LP	*Listening Post*
LZ	*Landing Zone*
MASCAL	*Mass Casualty Situation*
M-ATV	*Mine Resistant Ambush Protected-All Terrain Vehicle*
M-ATVs	*MRAP-All Terrain Vehicles*
MEDCAP	*Medical Civic Assistance Programs*
MEDEVAC	*Medical Evacuation*
MGS	*Mobile Gun System*
MICLIC	*Mine Clearing Line Charge*

MOLLE	Modular Lightweight Load-Carrying Equipment
MP	Military Police
MRAP	Mine Resistant Ambush Protected
MREs	Meals Ready to Eat
MTOE	Modified Table of Organization and Equipment
NAIs	Named Area of Interest
NCO	Non-Commissioned Officer
NCOIC	Non-Commissioned Officer In Charge
NGO	Nongovernmental Organizations
NODs	Night Observation Devices
NVGs	Night Vision Goggles
OEF	Operation ENDURING FREEDOM
OHDACA	Overseas Humanitarian, Disaster, and Civic Aid
OP	Observation Post
OP-FET	Operational FET
OPSEC	Operational Security
PCI	Pre-Combat Inspection
PRTs	Provincial Reconstruction Teams
QRF	Quick Reaction Force
RC	Regional Command
RCP	Route Clearance Package
RIP	Relief in Place
RPG	Rocket-Propelled Grenades
RTO	Radio Telephone Operator
SAW	Squad Automatic Weapon
SOF	Special Operations Forces
SRT	Special Reaction Team
TAA	Tactical Assembly Area
TAC-FET	Tactical FET
TBI	Traumatic Brain Injury
TF	Task Force
TOC	Tactical Operations Center
UAV	Unmanned Aerial Vehicle

UNAMA   *United Nations Assistance Mission in Afghanistan*
USAID   *United States Agency for International Development*
WIA   *Wounded in Action*
XO   *Executive Officer*

About the Authors

Anthony E. Carlson holds a Ph.D. in History from the University of Oklahoma. He currently serves as an historian on the Afghan Study Team at the Combat Studies Institute and an adjunct Assistant Professor of History for the US Army Command and General Staff College. His publications include works on Progressive Era US water and flood control policy, public works, and the antebellum Army Corps of Topographical Engineers.

Michael J. Doidge is a Doctoral Candidate at the University of Southern Mississippi, where he co-edited Triumph Revisited: Historians Battle for the Vietnam War. In addition to writing his dissertation, Michael currently serves as an Army historian on the Afghan Study Team at the Combat Studies Institute and an adjunct Assistant Professor of History for the US Army Command and General Staff College.

Scott J. Gaitley holds a MA in Military History from Norwich University. He is the author of Ambushing the Taliban: A US Platoon in the Korengal Valley published in volume one of Vanguard of Valor: Small Unit Actions in Afghanistan. Before serving on the Afghan Study Team at the Combat Studies Institute, he served as an Air Force Wing Historian in both Iraq and Afghanistan and more recently as a staff historian at the Air Force Reserve Command Headquarters.

Kevin M. Hymel holds an MA in History from Villanova University. He is the author of Patton's Photographs: War As He Saw It and coauthor of Patton: Legendary World War II Commander, with Martin Blumenson. Before serving on the Afghan Study Team at the Combat Studies Institute, he worked for a number of military and military history magazines as a researcher, editor, and writer.

Matt M. Matthews has worked at the Combat Studies Institute since July 2005 and is currently a member of the Afghan Study Team. He is the author of numerous CSI publications. Mr. Matthews has also co-authored various scholarly articles on the Civil War in the trans-Mississippi. He is a frequent speaker at Civil War Roundtables and the former Mayor of Ottawa, Kansas.

Ryan D. Wadle received a Ph.D. in History from Texas A&M University. He currently serves as an historian on the Afghan Study Team at the US Army Combat Studies Institute. In addition to his official duties, he is currently working on an article-length study of joint Army-Navy training and doctrine in the interwar period.

www.ingramcontent.com/pod-product-compliance
Lightning Source LLC
Chambersburg PA
CBHW050501110426
42742CB00018B/3331